To:

————THE————
WILDFLOWER GARDENER'S
————GUIDE————

California, Desert Southwest, and Northern Mexico Edition

you make
such a
difference

V.

THE WILDFLOWER GARDENER'S GUIDE

California, Desert Southwest, and Northern Mexico Edition

HENRY W. ART

Botanical illustrations by Hyla M. Skudder
Garden illustrations by Elayne Sears
Photographs by the author

STOREY

A Garden Way Publishing Book
Storey Communications, Inc.
Pownal, Vermont 05261

Cover photograph of blazing star (Mentzelia lindleyi) *and farewell-to-spring*
  (Clarkia amoena) *by Henry W. Art*
Book design by Andrea Gray
Edited by Deborah Burns
Maps rendered by Northern Cartographic, Inc.
Typesetting by Accura Type & Design, Barre, Vermont
Printed in the United States by Alpine Press

Copyright ©1990 by Storey Communications, Inc.

The name Garden Way Publishing has been licensed to Storey Communications, Inc. by Garden Way, Inc.

First printing, January 1990

Library of Congress Cataloging-in-Publication Data

Art, Henry Warren.
  The wildflower gardener's guide. California, Desert Southwest,
and northern Mexico edition / Henry W. Art ; botanical illustrations
by Hyla M. Skudder; garden illustrations by Elayne Sears ;
photographs by the author.
  Includes bibliographical references.
  ISBN 0-88266-564-2 : $22.95. — ISBN 0-88266-565-0 (pbk.) : $12.95
    1. Wild flower gardening—Southwest, New. 2. Wild flower
gardening—California. 3. Wild flower gardening—Mexico. 4. Wild
flowers—Southwest, New. 5. Wild flowers—California. 6. Wild
flowers—Mexico.   I. Title.
SB439.24.S68A78 1990
635.9'676'0979—dc20   89-45741
                                                                              CIP

This book is dedicated to
Mandy, Willy, Rick, Gwen, Devin, Daniel, and Nancy
Some native, some transplants, all favorites.

Contents

Acknowledgments

The author would like to thank the following people:

Melanie Bear and Dennis Bryson of the Theodore Payne Foundation, for too many things to enumerate.

Nancy and Rick Art, Jinx and Curt Tong, Bruce Mahall, and James Art, for their hospitality and good cheer.

Bob Haller, Jeanette Sainz, and Roger Raiche, for assistance in scouting sites for wildflower photography.

Jim Affolter and Roger Raiche of the University of California Botanic Garden, and John Taylor of Flagstaff, Arizona, for helpful assistance on botanical issues.

Amy King and Walter Wisura, of the Rancho Santa Ana Botanic Garden, Barrett Anderson of the Strybing Arboretum and Botanical Garden, and Dara Emery of the Santa Barbara Botanic Garden, for their help and support.

David Shea of the Williams College Library, for computer literature searches.

Deborah Burns, for continued sensitive editing and the ability to turn carpentry into cabinetwork.

Martha and John Storey, and Pam Art, for continued vision and encouragement.

Hundreds of people from the botanic gardens, nature centers, arboreta, wildflower seed companies, native plant nurseries, native plant societies, and botanical organizations, who responded to requests for the information contained in the appendices; and to Kim Foster and Jamie Art for their assistance in gathering this data.

THE
WILDFLOWER GARDENER'S
GUIDE

California, Desert Southwest, and Northern Mexico Edition

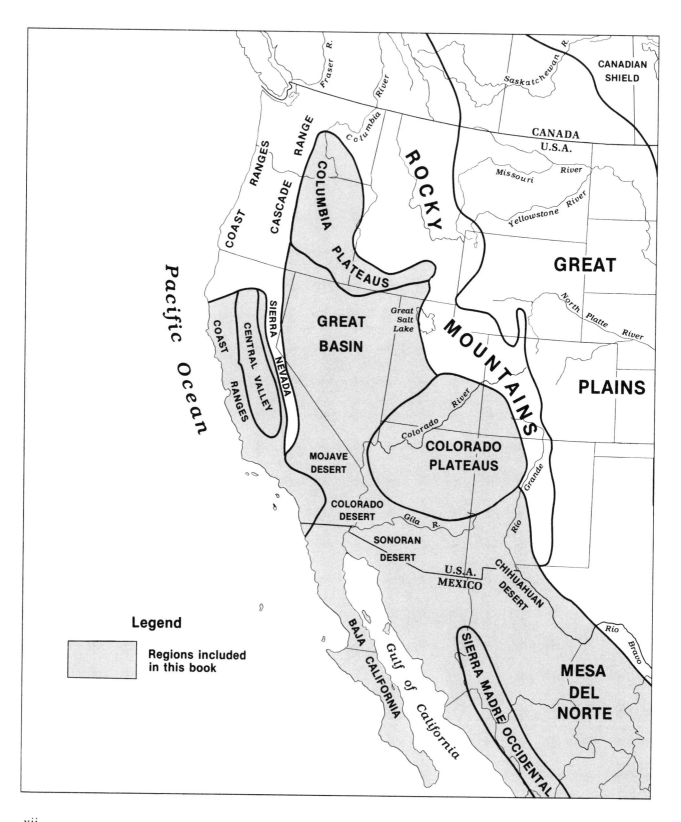

Pacific Ocean

COAST RANGES

CASCADE RANGE

COLUMBIA PLATEAUS

Fraser R.

Columbia River

ROCKY

CANADIAN
SHIELD

Saskatchewan R.

CANADA
U.S.A.

Missouri River

Yellowstone River

GREAT

SIERRA NEVADA

COAST RANGES

CENTRAL VALLEY

GREAT
BASIN

Great
Salt
Lake

MOUNTAINS

North Platte River

PLAINS

MOJAVE
DESERT

Colorado River

COLORADO
PLATEAUS

COLORADO
DESERT

SONORAN
DESERT

Gila R.

U.S.A.
MEXICO

CHIHUAHUAN
DESERT

Rio Grande

Rio

Legend

Regions included
in this book

BAJA CALIFORNIA

Gulf of California

SIERRA MADRE OCCIDENTAL

Rio Bravo

**MESA
DEL
NORTE**

PART I

An Introduction for Wildflower Gardeners

This book is about growing wildflowers in the southwestern corner of North America, a region extending from Mexico through the deserts of New Mexico and Arizona, north through the Great Basin — Utah, Nevada, Idaho and eastern Oregon — to eastern Washington and west to coastal California. This edition of *The Wildflower Gardener's Guide* focuses on the region below 6,000 feet in elevation and includes a variety of habitats, ranging from deserts to grasslands to chaparral to foothill woodlands. Of the hundreds of wildflowers that grow in these habitats, 34 of the most easily cultivated and beautiful species have been selected for inclusion in this book. These wildflowers have been chosen to cover the range of flowering season and garden conditions typical of southwestern North America below the montane zone.

Wildflowers of Southwestern North America

Enjoying wildflowers in the Southwest may seem a bit like enjoying fine wines: some years produce vintages that are remembered long after the pleasure is gone, and other years produce merely hope for the future. While the climate that influences the showy wildflower displays may be variable from year to year, a real joy of gardening in the Southwest is turning environmental challenges into opportunities. You can incorporate the spectacular diversity of native species into your personal landscape — be it containers on a balcony, a modest yard, or a considerable ranch.

The Southwest is blessed with a diversity of environmental conditions that make it an exciting landscape to live in. Less than 90 miles separate Mt. Whitney, at 14,495 feet above sea level the highest point in the conterminous U.S., and Bad Water, the lowest point in North America at 279 feet below sea level. Between the extremes of the Sierra Nevada range and Death Valley are perhaps a wider variety of habitats than are found anywhere else on this continent. The dramatic topography of the region, equally dramatic seasonal climatic changes, and a complex geologic history have contributed to the impressive diversity of native plants that inhabit these environments.

The seasonal extremes of the Southwest, with hot winds, torrential rains, periodic fires, and parched soils, can be hard on conventional gardens. Wildflowers provide solutions to many gardening problems since, unlike most domesticated, horticultural plants, they have the ability to make it on their own without human assistance.

WILDFLOWER HABITATS

The native wildflowers of the Southwest are the products of their varied habitats. The region today is quite different from the Southwest of four centuries ago when the Spanish started to colonize Mexico. European settlement brought not only horses, cattle, and sheep but also a vast new array of plants that found the environment to their liking. Some of these plants were introduced by farmers and ranchers to produce food and fodder, while other Old World weeds got here by accident. Black mustard, on the other hand, with its bright, sulfur yellow flowers, appears to have been planted on coastal hillsides by the Spanish to mark the entrances to harbors.

Over the centuries the vast interior grassland of California's Central Valley was transformed by these Old World plants and animals until today little native grassland vegetation survives. Even the foothills, chaparral, and desert areas have been highly modified by human activities in the region. Nevertheless, amid the current patchwork of cities, suburbs, countryside, ranches, and farm fields are the remnants of the plant communities that have nurtured these wildflowers for millions of years.

Deserts. Parts of the area covered in this book — much of eastern California through New Mexico and north to Washington — have less than 10 inches of precipitation annually. Not only is there scant rainfall, but its amount and frequency vary greatly from year to year. Plants growing in the desert often endure stretches of prolonged drought punctuated by brief periods of "too much" water.

Desert temperatures may also vary widely. The Mojave, Colorado, Sonoran and Chihuahan deserts below 3,000 feet in elevation have very hot summers and cool winters. The deserts of the Great Basin above 4,000 feet in elevation, on the other hand, are known as "cold deserts," not because their summers are much cooler, but because their winter temperatures are generally below freezing. Most of the precipitation in the Great Basin desert is snow, while in the hot deserts it is rain — winter rains in California and summer thunderstorms in Arizona and New Mexico. Summer daytime humidity is generally extremely low in both hot and cold deserts, and water evaporates quickly.

It is no surprise that desert plants have evolved techniques of conserving moisture during droughty periods and can quickly take advantage of water when it is available. Many of the shrubs that dominate the Great Basin, such as sagebrush, shadscale, and bitter bush, have light-colored foliage that reflect the sun. The ocotillo, palo verde, and brittle bush of the hot deserts shed their leaves and go into dormancy during drought, while succulent plants like cacti endure drought by drawing upon their reserves of water absorbed during the brief rains. The annual desert wildflowers such as desert sand verbena, California bluebells, and desert marigold avoid drought by completing their entire life cycles in short bursts when water is available, producing seeds that remain viable even when kept dry for years. The spectacular shows of annual wildflowers when the desert blooms usually occur during a year with abundant rainfall ending a period of several dry years.

Grasslands. The vast floor of California's Central Valley once supported grasslands that were lush green in the spring and turned golden yellow in the summer. Now the Valley supports much of California's agriculture. The native perennial bunch grasses, such as needle grass, Indian rice grass, tufted hair grass, and three-awn, have been replaced by non-native pasture or hay grasses and irrigated agriculture.

The native grasses owed their presence to the combination of minimal rainfall — less than 20 inches of rain every winter — and very dry summers. In addition, frequent fires prevented the encroachment of trees and shrubs from the Coast Ranges and Sierra Nevada foothills, which encircle the Central Valley. The native grasses and numerous wildflowers, such as California poppy, tidy tips, goldfields, purple annual lupine, owl's clover, and farewell-to-spring, start their growth during the cool wet winter and either enter dormancy or end their life cycles by producing seeds by the start of the summer drought. Similar patches of natural grassland known as "coastal prairie" are found on south- and west-facing slopes and bluffs of mountains near the Pacific Ocean, and "desert grasslands" are found on the wetter, upslope margins of deserts in the Southwest. In grasslands as in deserts, a mild wet winter following a series of dry winters will trigger the blooming of masses of spring wildflowers.

Chaparral. Rocky, craggy, well-drained slopes near the Pacific Ocean, and occasionally inland, are frequently covered with thick, often deep-rooted, fire-adapted shrubs known collectively as *chaparral*. Like grasslands, the chaparral is found in areas with a Mediterranean-type climate of cool, wet winters and warm, dry summers. The driest sites are usually dominated by various species of sage, coastal sagebrush, and other low shrubby species that comprise a type of vegetation known as "coastal sage scrub" or "soft chaparral." "Hard chaparral," on the other hand, is found on wetter sites and is dominated by evergreen shrubs such as chamise, manzanita, and ceanothus (California lilac), as well as many beautiful wildflowers such as golden yarrow, prickly poppy, Douglas's wallflower, showy penstemon, and Our Lord's candle, which punctuate the olive drab landscape with springtime color.

Fire plays a dominant role in maintaining this type of vegetation, and a given patch of chaparral is likely to burn every 20 years or so. The fires usually occur during the summer and autumn dry season, especially when hot Santa Ana winds blow out of the interior deserts and head downslope toward the sea. The rainy season follows the fire season, and often the thin chaparral soils are further impoverished by erosion.

Chaparral species are far from devastated by fire; in fact most are stimulated by periodic burning. Chamise resprouts vigorously after being burnt, while the seeds of ceanothus and even some wildflowers like prickly poppy have enhanced germination in response to the heat of the fire. Fire may also cleanse the soil of the accumulated plant toxins exuded by many of the chaparral shrubs.

North Coastal Forests. Evergreen forests are found along the Pacific Coast north of the chaparral zone, where the climate tends to be more moist, if not wet, and the ocean still maintains mild temperatures year-round. Here the coast redwoods, the tallest trees in the world, mingle with Douglas fir, western hemlock, sitka spruce, lowland fir and other conifers, and even some deciduous species such as bigleaf maple. The wildflowers of this type of forest, which extends northward along the coast into Canada, are presented in the Northwestern Edition of *The Wildflower Gardener's Guide*.

Foothill Woodlands. Inland areas that are moister and less fire prone than chaparral or grasslands frequently have open woodlands with scattered evergreen and deciduous oaks, California buckeye, digger pine, and California walnut. In desert regions of the Southwest, the cooler, moister sites at higher elevations are frequently dominated by oaks, piñon pine, and juniper. Often adjacent chaparral or grasslands intergrade with the woodlands that surround them and share many of the same wildflower species. Some of the foothill woodland wildflowers, such as Chinese houses and baby blue-eyes, grow best in the filtered shade of trees rather than in constant sunlight. Others, such as Douglas's iris and giant evening primrose, thrive on the additional moisture found in this habitat.

Montane Vegetation. Much of the Sierra Nevada range extends above 6,000 feet in elevation and its wildflowers, like those of the Cascade Range and Rocky Mountains, are presented in the Northwestern Edition of *The Wildflower Gardener's Guide*. These regions typically receive at least 40 inches of precipitation, mostly in the form of snow.

In the Sierra Nevada giant sequoias, the largest organisms on earth, and ponderosa or yellow pines are usually found in the zone between 6,000 and 8,000 feet, while above 8,000 feet red fir, Jeffrey pine, and lodgepole pine are frequently dominant. Near the timberline white fir, Jeffrey pine and, especially, whitebark pine usually increase in importance, but decrease in height. The conditions in the treeless alpine meadows and rocky "fell fields" above the timberline are so harsh that the tallest plants are dwarf shrubs and tufted cushion plants.

THE JOYS OF WILDFLOWERS

The beauty of southwestern wildflowers has long captivated botanists and gardeners from around the world. Spanish, Russian and, especially, British plant explorers became enthralled with the new wildflowers they found in this corner of the New World and eagerly introduced them to Europe in the 18th and 19th centuries. Many of the Latin and common names of southwestern wildflowers reveal the enchantment they held for European botanists like Archibald

Menzies, Johann Friedrich Eschscholz, and David Douglas. Douglas, in whose honor Douglas fir, Douglas's wallflower, and Douglas's iris were named, visited California several times in the 1830s on missions for the Horticultural Society of London. California poppy, sky lupine, Chinese houses, purple heliotrope, farewell-to-spring, blazing star, baby blue-eyes, and linanthus were among his discoveries and soon graced British gardens.

Modern-day gardeners can share the botanists' fascination by introducing wildflowers into their own gardens — and even the most common of native species can bring great pleasure as one learns their secrets.

Our Lord's candle. The pollination of Our Lord's candle is a fascinating story. The plant starts to flower as its only pollinator, the yucca moth (*Tegeticula maculata*), emerges in the spring. The fragrant white flowers open in the evening when the moth is most active. A female moth visits a flower and, with her specialized mouth parts, scrapes the pollen, rolls it up into a ball about three times the size of her head, and flies with it to another newly opened flower. She backs down to the base of the pistil, injects her eggs into the ovary of the plant, and then crawls up to the stigmatic surface. Here she carefully attaches the mass of pollen, ensuring both the fertilization of the flower and the production of seeds. The growing larvae consume some of the seeds, but burrow out of the fruit and into the ground before the pod shatters and seeds are released. Adult moths emerge from the ground the next spring during the flowering season, completing the life cycle. Neither Our Lord's candle nor the species of yucca moth that pollinates it can reproduce without the other.

Other species. A wildflower garden may have other delights awaiting discovery. The flowers of the California poppy change subtly from hour to hour and from spring to fall. They emerge after pushing off a small green cap known as a *calyptra*. Each day the blossoms open wide in the morning sun and close up during the evening. This short-lived perennial produces large, bright orange flowers in the early spring and smaller, yellow-orange ones later in the season.

Other species have intriguing stories as well. Giant evening primrose flowers open at sunset and turn from yellow to orange as they wither in the next day's afternoon sun. The fruits of sky lupine explode, shooting out the seeds as they ripen. Owl's clover frequently obtains some of its nourishment by parasitizing the roots of other nearby wildflowers and grasses.

This book presents but a few of the hundreds of wildflowers that are worthy of introduction into gardens in southwestern North America. Although some of us greatly enjoy studying those intricacies of wildflower life cycles that can be discovered only through close observation, others may be perfectly content simply appreciating the subtle colors and graceful forms of these elements of our natural heritage.

Getting a Start

This book presents 34 wildflowers native to southwestern North American woodlands and meadows. You may already be familiar with some of these species, such as California poppy, baby blue-eyes, and tidy tips, and others such as lomatium may be new to you. The selected species are well adapted to the range of conditions likely to exist in gardens of the region and can be propagated without much difficulty. Although any wildflower becomes scarce near the edges of its natural range, none of the species included in this book is designated "rare" or "endangered." They are available from reputable wildflower suppliers who sell nursery-propagated stock, or from seed companies.

It is delightful to watch the parade of wildflowers through the growing season, and the species chosen for this edition will provide a succession of flowering from late winter through autumn. These wildflowers can be grown in a wide variety of conditions, from conventional gardens to woodlands, from meadows to deserts; some can even be grown in containers on your porch or patio. Hopefully, the wildflowers in this book will be only a starting point for your gardening with native plants. There are many other species presented in other regional editions of *The Wildflower Gardener's Guide*, *A Garden of Wildflowers*, and other books on native-plant gardening suitable for southwestern North American gardens.

Some wildflowers, not included in this book, are difficult to bring into the garden because of their demanding soil or cultural requirements. Snowplant lacks chlorophyll, for example, and therefore must parasitize the roots of other plants in order to survive. The Indian paintbrushes, which do have green leaves, are nevertheless parasitic on the roots of other plants, and nearly impossible to cultivate in a garden. The mariposa lilies have not been included, because they are generally difficult to grow and because a considerable number of *Calochortus* species are relatively rare. They are best left growing where they are in the wild and should be moved into your garden only if they are in imminent danger of destruction by development.

Wildflower Conservation Guidelines*

1. Let your acts reflect your respect for wild native plants as integral parts of biological communities and natural landscapes. Remember that if you pick a wildflower, your action affects the natural world, and that the cumulative effects of the actions of many people can be particularly harmful.

2. Do not collect native plants or plant parts from the wild except as part of rescue operations sponsored by responsible organizations.

3. Encourage the use of regional native plants in home and public landscapes, but before obtaining wildflower plants or seeds for your home landscape, learn enough about their cultural requirements to be sure you can provide a suitable habitat.

4. If you collect seeds from the wild, collect a few seeds or fruits from each of many plants and *only from common species that are locally abundant.* Purchase wildflower seeds only from companies that collect responsibly.

5. Purchase live wildflower plants only from suppliers or organizations that *propagate* their own plants or that purchase their material from those who propagate them. Ask sellers about the origin of the plants you are considering buying. If there is any doubt about a plant's origin, do not purchase it.

6. Be cautious and knowledgeable in the use of exotic wildflowers. While many non-native species can be attractively used in gardens and landscapes, some are overly aggressive and these weeds may displace native species. Become aware of your state's noxious weed laws by contacting your state Department of Agriculture or Agricultural Extension Service.

7. When photographing wildflowers, or inspecting them closely, be careful not to trample plants nearby.

8. If you pick wildflowers, dried seed stalks, or greens for home decoration, use only common species that are abundant at the site. Leave enough flowers or seeds to allow the plant population to reseed itself. Avoid picking herbaceous perennials such as wild orchids, mariposa lilies, or gentians which, like daffodils, need to retain their vegetative parts to store energy for next year's development. Avoid cutting slow-growing plants such as cacti.

9. Become familiar with your state's wildflower protection laws. If your state does not have laws protecting wildflowers, or if the existing laws are weak, support the passage and enforcement of strong and effective legislation for the preservation of native plants. Report unlawful collection of plants to proper authorities and, when necessary, remind others that collecting plants or disturbing a natural area is illegal in parks and other public places.

10. If you learn that an area with wildflowers is scheduled for development, notify a native plant society in your region. Discuss with the developer the possibilities of compatible development alternatives or of conducting a wildflower rescue operation.

11. It is important to protect information about the locations of rare species. If you discover a new site of a plant species that you know is rare, report it to responsible conservation officials, such as your state's Natural Heritage Program, a native plant society, a Nature Conservancy chapter, or the U.S. Fish and Wildlife Service, as soon as possible and before discussing it with others.

*Adapted from the Virginia Wildflower Preservation Society's "Wildflower Conservation Guidelines."

WILDFLOWER CONSERVATION

One safeguard of our native wild plants is the Federal Endangered Species Act of 1973, administered by the U.S. Fish and Wildlife Service. This act gives protection to those native species that are recognized as endangered in the United States. This law applies only to federal lands, however, and to the interstate traffic of rare plants. The protection of endangered wildflowers on other public and private lands is left up to the states, as is the protection of species that might become locally rare or endangered through collection by native-plant suppliers and wildflower fanciers. State laws protecting wildflowers are far from uniform, and even where there is protective legislation, the enforcement of these laws is sometimes weak.

Wildflower gardeners should become aware of their state's laws concerning the protection of native plants. If your state lacks such protective legislation, or if the enforcement of the laws is weak, become an advocate for passage of strong and effective measures. The World Wildlife Fund and the Environmental Defense Fund, whose addresses can be found in Appendix C, can provide information concerning model native-plant protection legislation.

The wildflower gardener is faced with moral and ethical considerations that do not confront the gardener of cultivars. Essential to the enjoyment and appreciation of wild, native plants is the respect for living organisms in their native habitats. The wildflower gardener's code of conduct should protect naturally occurring populations of native plants, not only so that others can enjoy them, but also to preserve the ecological roles these plants play. Individual actions do make a difference, both positively and negatively. Wildflower gardeners have the chance to counteract the tragedy of habitat destruction and reduction in native-plant populations occurring around the world.

PLANTING STOCK

One of the first questions one might ask is where to obtain seeds or plants to start a garden of wildflowers. Where not to obtain plants is easier to answer. *Plants growing in their native habitats should never be dug up for the garden.* Apart from the laws that protect wildflowers in many states, it is unethical to uproot native plants. Furthermore, many deeply rooted perennials are nearly impossible to transplant even with a backhoe.

The propagation instructions given for the 34 species of wildflowers in this book are intended for gardeners who desire to make divisions of their own plants only, not of those growing in the wild. The only circumstance in which it is acceptable to dig up wildflowers is when they are imminently threatened by highway development or construction. In those cases, prior approval must be obtained from the proper authorities, and if possible, plants should be dug while dormant.

Nursery-grown material usually yields the best wildflower gardening results. Before ordering plants by mail or from a local retail outlet, determine whether the plants have been propagated in a nursery, not merely "grown" there for a while. Do not buy plants that have been collected in the wild, since this practice may deplete natural populations of plants deserving protection. When ordering wildflowers you may wish to purchase seeds or live plants from a producer who is relatively close by, since there is a greater likelihood that the stock is better adapted to your local environmental conditions.

Seeds. Much can be gained by propagating wildflowers by seed, even apart from their year-round availability, durability in shipping, and relatively low cost. Raising wildflowers from seed gives the gardener a chance to become familiar with the complete life cycle of plants. Some of the species in this book will self-seed once established, and therefore it is useful to know from firsthand experience what the seedlings of the species look like. Often the leaves of seedlings look different from those of mature plants, and without this knowledge they might be accidently removed as weeds.

You can collect the seeds of most perennials growing in the wild without fear of significantly affecting their populations, if you take only a small proportion of the seeds that are produced. Since annuals reproduce only by seed, you should collect seeds from them only in locations where their populations are abundant. Before collecting any seeds get permission from the property owner.

Wildflower seeds are usually available throughout the year from mail-order suppliers. Some perennial wildflowers of southwestern North America have enhanced germination when their seeds are chilled or *stratified* for several months. Check with the supplier to determine whether the seeds you purchase have been pretreated or if they would benefit from additional cold treatment.

Wildflower Seed Mixtures: Caution! You should be very cautious and fully informed before purchasing commercial wildflower seed mixtures, which recently have been gaining popularity. Some suppliers painstakingly formulate mixtures that are representative of native wildflowers of specific regions or habitats. Others, however, formulate mixes for broad geographic regions and may include species that are not particularly adapted to your local conditions. Furthermore, it is often difficult to know just what species are contained in some of the mixtures and in what proportions. Some of the producers of the wildflower mixtures will vary the composition depending upon the temporary availability of seeds, so there is no guarantee that the product will be uniform from year to year. Often the mixes contain an abundance of annuals that provide a splash of color the first year but have difficulty in reseeding themselves. The lack of perennials in these mixes may mean disappointment in subsequent years. As long as you are investing in wildflowers, you might as well pay for only what you want, not just a pretty can or a packet mostly of roadside weeds.

A further difficulty with some of the mixes is the inclusion of weedy, non-native wildflower species which, while attractive, may become aggressive. An analysis by the New England Wild Flower Society of various wildflower seed mixes in 1985 found them to be comprised of eight to thirty-four different species, of which zero to 100 percent were native. The following are some non-native species that are commonly found in wildflower mixes:

SPECIES	PLACE OF ORIGIN	SPECIES	PLACE OF ORIGIN
Oxeye daisy	Europe	Dame's rocket	France
Corn poppy	Europe	African daisy	South Africa
Sweet alyssum	Europe–W. Asia	Foxglove	Europe
White yarrow	Europe	Candytuft	S.E. Europe– W. Asia
Baby's breath	S. Europe	Four-o'clock	Peru
Purple loosestrife	N. Europe	Queen Anne's lace	Europe
St. John's-wort	Europe–Africa	Chicory	Europe
Bouncing bet	Europe–Asia	Cornflower	Europe

Live Plants. Since it often takes several years for perennial wildflowers to bloom when started from seed, the fastest way to establish them in the garden is to purchase live plants from reputable suppliers. Planning is essential. Perennial wildflowers are best shipped and planted when they are dormant. Many mail-order suppliers ship only during a limited season, so you should contact suppliers to determine the season of availability and whether there are any other constraints in shipping the specific live wildflowers you wish to plant.

SUPPLIERS   The number of reputable commercial producers and distributors of wildflower plants and seeds is steadily increasing, especially in metropolitan areas of the Southwest. Some commercial sources are listed in Appendix A, although their inclusion is in no way an endorsement by the author or publisher. Most suppliers have catalogs or lists giving prices of seeds, live plants, and other items useful in wildflower gardening. Many of these catalogs are extremely useful sources of information about growing native plants. As is noted in Appendix A, some of the suppliers have a small charge for their catalogs and some refund that charge with the first order. It is a good idea to order catalogs several months in advance of your anticipated planting time. Some suppliers have shipping restrictions across international boundaries, and where these are known they are mentioned in Appendix A. Most suppliers prefer payment in the currency of their own country, and some require it.

If you are planning to plant large areas with mature bulbs and rootstocks, some of the suppliers listed in Appendix A sell large quantities of live plants (and seeds) to the public at wholesale prices. Although many suppliers give wholesale discounts to the public, some sell at wholesale rates only to registered retailers, so check with the supplier first.

MORE INFORMATION

This book may be just a beginning for you. Further information is available from many sources, some of which are listed in the appendices to this book.

Botanical Gardens. Botanical gardens, nature centers, and arboreta are excellent sources of information about gardening with native plants. A state-by-state listing of such institutions is given in Appendix B. This listing includes the admission fee, if any, the season of operation, and the phone numbers. The resources of these gardens and centers usually extend beyond their collections of living native plants. Many offer workshops, symposia, tours, or lecture series on wildflower gardening. Some publish magazines, newsletters, and brochures that include information on native plants, and they often have shops that sell books on wildflowers as well as wildflower seeds and live plants.

Many botanical gardens offer memberships that entitle members to use library facilities, attend special events at reduced prices, go on field trips to various natural areas, consult with the horticultural staff, use a phone "gardening hotline," and enjoy other benefits. If you become interested in the institution's activities, they may have a program in which you could become a volunteer.

There are numerous other places not listed in Appendix B to observe wildflowers. Many local, regional, state, and national parks have preserved areas of native vegetation. National Forests and National Wildlife Refuges are also ideal places to see native wildflowers, as are lands owned by various chapters of the Audubon Society and the Nature Conservancy.

Botanical Organizations. Native plant societies and some horticultural organizations are excellent sources of information about native plants, as well as a means of becoming involved with wildflowers. The activities and resources of these societies are quite varied, ranging from projects to conserve rare and endangered plants to field trips, lecture series, and seed exchanges. Many of the native plant societies periodically publish newsletters or bulletins and have smaller local chapters that hold regular meetings. Some of the societies are affiliated with specific botanic gardens or arboreta, while others have a more regional or national focus. Appendix C lists botanical organizations that are concerned with wildflowers.

One organization concerned with native plants across the continent is the National Wildflower Research Center, located in Austin, Texas. The N.W.R.C., founded in 1982, is a clearinghouse for wildflower information, an institution conducting research on the propagation and cultivation of native plants, and an advocate for wildflower conservation and preservation. The public is encouraged both to contact the N.W.R.C. for information about native plants and to join them in their cause. The address of the National Wildflower Research Center is given in Appendix C.

On a state level, most states in the southwestern United States have Natural Heritage Programs, cooperative efforts between the Nature Conservancy and state departments of fish and game or natural resources to take inventory of rare plants, animals, and biological communities. The first Natural Heritage Program was started in South Carolina in 1974, to provide that state with biological inventory data augmenting the Federal Endangered Species Act. The offices of Natural Heritage Programs listed in Appendix C can provide you with current information on rare and endangered wildflowers and plant communities in your state.

The National Council of State Garden Clubs, Inc. is also active in wildflower preservation, and advocates using native plants for landscaping roadsides and public spaces. The organization sponsors "Operation Wildflower," a cooperative effort among state garden club federations, state highway agencies, and the Federal Highway Administration to beautify the nation's highways with native species, providing a low-cost, low-maintenance alternative to the exotic grasses and weeds that dominate our roadsides. Since its inception in 1972, Operation Wildflower has extended its horizons beyond the roadside to include projects in public parks, gardens, and wildflower preserves.

References. An annotated bibliography of books and published resources on wildflower gardening is contained in Appendix D.

Theme Gardens

Cultivating native wildflowers of southwestern North America can open new horizons in low-maintenance gardening. A sense of satisfaction accompanies the reestablishment of plants that were once more widespread in the region. Whether you use native plants to complement existing gardens or establish new plantings of species with different environmental requirements, you don't have to start out on a grand scale. Some of the most successful wildflower gardens are small flower beds at the corner of a house or on small patches of land otherwise unused. Even those areas you can't mow anyway between the roots of the trees in the front yard can be enhanced by plantings of wildflowers.

Wildflowers let you adapt landscapes for specific purposes, such as "xeriscaping" to reduce water consumption by planting drought-tolerant plants, and "firescaping" to reduce the possible loss of buildings by planting fire-resistant species. Wildflowers can also be used in more natural settings. Foothill woodlands can be enhanced through the addition of wildflowers adapted to that habitat. Similarly, you can beautify desert, grassland, and chaparral areas by planting appropriate species of native wildflowers.

HORTICULTURAL GARDENS

Beds and Borders. The simplest approach is to use wildflowers in existing gardens to complement your ornamental plants. Conventional flower beds might include species such as Douglas's wallflower, Chinese houses, baby blue-eyes, and California poppy. Farewell-to-spring, Douglas's iris, blue dicks, and coralbells should also be considered, because their long stems and long-lasting flowers make them ideal cut flowers.

Many southwestern native plants are ideal for sunny borders. Tidy tips, linanthus, goldfields, California bluebell, sky lupine, and owl's clover, with their low growth forms and interesting foliage, make excellent border plants. If your border is shady, try western shooting star, baby blue-eyes, and Chinese houses.

Butterfly and Hummingbird Gardens. If you want to attract butterflies to your garden, plant species such as Douglas's wallflower, blue dicks, Douglas's iris, purple heliotrope, and tidy tips, which have contrasting flower colors or produce sweet nectars that attract the adult butterflies. Another approach is to plant wildflowers that the developing caterpillars like to eat. The larvae of small butterflies known as "blues" eat lupines as their main food, and West Coast lady butterflies eat checker bloom and other members of the mallow family. One obvious reason to refrain from using insecticides in wildflower gardens is the harm they cause to butterflies.

Hummingbirds are attracted to red or pink flowers that point outward or hang down. To lure hummingbirds to your garden, try planting coralbells, California fuchsia, and Eaton's firecracker. These wildflowers, planted as companions to those that attract butterflies, will provide a long season of winged guests.

Ground Covers. Some of the native species in this book make superb ground covers and are effective in controlling erosion. To stabilize sunny banks and steep areas prone to erosion, plant perennials such as California fuchsia, showy penstemon, Eaton's firecracker, and lomatium, with its deep and spreading roots, along with native grasses and shrubs. Southwestern verbena and desert sand verbena make attractive temporary ground covers for areas that aren't subjected to foot traffic. Under the proper conditions these annuals will even reseed.

A. Douglas's iris
B. Blue dicks
C. Farewell-to-spring
D. Chinese houses
E. Checker bloom
F. Eaton's firecracker
G. Coralbells

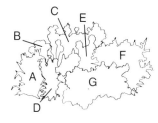

Hummingbird and butterfly garden

Rock Gardens. No rock garden is truly complete without representative native species. By their very nature the species growing in the chaparral are adapted to rock garden conditions and are especially successful when you are "firescaping" or designing a fire-resistant garden. When using wildflowers you can create rock gardens for sun or shade, and for moist or dry conditions. Take the environmental preferences of various wildflowers into consideration when planning your rock garden. Plant desert marigold, Douglas's wallflower, lomatium, and farewell-to-spring in dry, sunny places such as the south-facing exposure near the top of the garden. Indian pink, on the other hand, prefers partial shade and relatively acid soils and might be planted on east- or west-facing slopes. Coralbells, checker bloom, and Chinese houses should be planted low on the north side of the rock garden so they can grow in partial shade and gain a bit more moisture than other rock garden plants. Western shooting star and blue-eyed grass can be grown in either full sun or partial shade, but should have ample moisture during their spring flowering season and then be allowed to dry out during the summer. If you have a large space for a rock garden you might consider growing more aggressive wildflowers like California fuchsia or larger species like Our Lord's candle.

A. Douglas's wallflower
B. Desert marigold
C. Farewell-to-spring
D. Indian pink
E. Chinese houses
F. Blue-eyed grass
G. Shooting star
H. Checker bloom

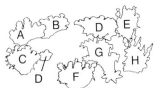

Wildflower rock garden

Container Gardening. Growing wildflowers in containers is an easy way to enjoy native plants if you live in a city, if your gardening space is limited, or if more intensive care is needed because your local conditions are quite different from those usually required by a particular species. One advantage to container gardening is that you can move the plants seasonally, indoors or out, to match the needs of the species. When wildflowers such as farewell-to-spring and Douglas's wallflower are planted densely in large containers they provide stunning accents for courtyards, balconies, or patios. Even Our Lord's candle can be grown in pots. Its hemispherical tuft of sword-shaped leaves will grow slowly for many years before it becomes too large for container gardening. Wooden or masonry boxes planted with the low-growing California bluebells or southwestern verbena are especially attractive along side paths and stairways.

Southwestern natives such as California fuchsia, desert sand verbena, or goldfields are well suited for growing in hanging baskets. All have interesting foliage, creeping stems that will grow to overflow the sides of baskets, and small attractive flowers of scarlet, pink, or yellow. Coralbells also make attractive potted plants when grown in low-profile, 8–12-inch containers.

A wide variety of containers can be used: conventional pots, wooden tubs, window boxes, hanging baskets, drainage tile, and chimney flue liners, to mention a few. Containers made of porous ceramic material, like clay pots, tend to dry out faster, so wildflowers planted in them need to be watered more frequently than those planted in impervious glass, glazed ceramic, or plastic containers.

Good drainage is essential for container gardening, since water-logged soils not only prevent the roots from getting needed oxygen, but also encourage diseases. Many plants adapted to dry soil conditions simply cannot tolerate wet soils. First, be sure the container has a drainage hole, and line the bottom of the pot with a layer of pot shards or gravel. The soil you use should be light and porous. Equal measures of top soil, peat moss, and builder's sand, mixed thoroughly, make a good potting mixture for most plants. With the plant in place, the pot should be filled to about 1 inch from the top with this loamy soil mix.

The root growth of plants in containers tends not to be as extensive as that of plants growing in conventional gardens, so additional water is usually required. Water the container garden only after the surface of the soil has become dry to the touch, and then water sufficiently for water to drain out and carry the dissolved salts out the drainage hole. Otherwise, salts may build up in the soil and damage the plants. Regular watering will remove some of the necessary plant nutrients from the soil, so periodically add small amounts of slow-release fertilizers to replace them.

NATURAL GARDENS AND LANDSCAPES

A highly successful way to use native plants is to plant wildflowers in appropriate natural settings. This also allows you to brighten up areas of your property that are difficult to plant, such as beaches, fire-prone areas, and dry, droughty spots. As a result your personal landscape will be adapted to its natural environment and require far less time, energy, and resources to maintain.

"Xeriscaping" — Gardening with Less Water. Xeriscaping is a new gardening and landscape approach gaining popularity in the arid Southwest as it becomes painfully obvious that water is an ever more scarce and expensive resource. The term "xeriscaping" is derived from the Greek word *xeros* meaning "dry," and is applied to techniques that reduce the water required to maintain gardens. The xeriscaping movement had its birth in the Denver area in the early 1980s. It gathered momentum later in the decade as cities like Los Angeles enacted ordinances requiring water-conserving landscaping for new industrial, commercial, and multi-family developments.

Xeriscaping stresses the establishment of landscapes adapted to the arid environments around them, rather than trying to transplant and maintain water-consumptive landscapes from the humid East or tropics. Included among the several techniques used to create water-thrifty gardens and landscapes are: reducing the areas devoted to lawns, planting water-conserving plants, using mulches where possible to conserve water, using soil amendments to increase the water-holding capacity of soils, grouping plants with similar water requirements close together, and, if absolutely needed, installing micro-irrigation systems that most efficiently meet the plants' water needs. Adopting these techniques can lead to a 30 to 80 percent reduction in water use compared to "humid" gardening in the Southwest.

In designing a xeriscape take advantage of the water draining from roofs, driveways, and impervious surfaces for supplemental irrigation. Also consider planting species with greater water needs in swales and depressions that collect rainwater at the beginning of the dry season. Even water-conserving species may need additional irrigation, but once established they should require only natural rainfall.

Native plants play a natural role in Southwestern xeriscapes, since they, above all species, are adapted to the local environment. The wildflowers presented in the sections on desert species (page 78) and chaparral species (page 118) are obvious candidates for water-conserving landscapes; however, several of the grassland species, such as California poppy, owl's clover, and wind poppy, are also quite drought tolerant. Trees and shrubs such as sagebrush (*Artemesia tridentata*), manzanita, flannel bush (*Fremontia californica*), buffaloberry (*Spherdia rotundifolia*), and bladderpod (*Isomeris arborea*) can also be used quite effectively in xeriscapes. Be sure to prune shrubs periodically so that they remain a manageable size, old wood is removed, and new vigorous growth is encouraged.

Container garden

A. Desert sand verbena
B. Goldfields
C. Douglas's wallflower
D. California bluebells
E. Southwestern verbena
F. Farewell-to-spring

Further information about xeriscaping is available from the Agricultural Extension Service, city or regional water authorities, botanic gardens, or the Xeriscaping Council, Inc., the address of which appears in Appendix C.

Chaparral Gardens and "Firescaping". Life in the chaparral region of southern and coastal California carries the recurring risk of fire sweeping across the landscape burning vegetation and structures alike. The native vegetation, for the most part, is adapted to coping with fires but the structures are not. While some native chaparral plants are highly flammable, many wildflowers can be effectively incorporated into "firescapes" or fire-resistant landscapes.

California state law (CA Resource Code 4219) requires homeowners to clear flammable, shrubby vegetation in a zone 30 to 100 feet around structures in fire hazard areas. The U.S. Forest Service and fire departments in chaparral areas are excellent sources of information concerning how to reduce the risks of brush fires. The Santa Barbara (California) Fire Department encourages home owners to design firescape plantings around their homes to reduce the danger of fire and the threat to property and even life.

A firescape typically consists of concentric zones around a house, starting with widely spaced fire-resistant species closest to the house. Next is a "green belt" of low-growing and succulent plants, such as cacti and live-forevers

Douglas's wallflower
Coralbells
Douglas's iris
Sky lupine
Purple annual lupine
Showy penstemon
Checker bloom
Blue-eyed grass
Desert mallow
California fuchsia

(*Dudleya* species), to a distance of about 100 feet. Beyond the green belt is a zone of slow-growing, relatively short, slow-burning plants such as the wildflowers listed in the chart at left. The final zone is native chaparral vegetation where the shrubs have been pruned to less than 7 feet in diameter, they have been thinned to stand about 20 feet apart, and they have had as much dead wood removed as possible. Dwarf coyote brush (*Baccharis pilularis* variety *pilularis*) and laurel sumac (*Rhus laurina* or *Malosma laurina*) are two low-growing shrubs that make excellent additions to this firescape zone.

Seaside Gardens. Some plants are difficult to grow in gardens exposed to fog and salt-laden winds coming off the Pacific Ocean. Many species of wildflowers, however, thrive in coastal areas and are naturally successful additions to the seaside garden. California poppy, blue-eyed grass, and desert sand verbena are among the first of the spring coastal species to bloom, followed closely by tidy tips, Douglas's iris, giant evening primrose, and checker bloom. Later, sky lupine and linanthus reach their peaks of flowering, and as the long days of summer approach, farewell-to-spring produces showy masses of pink and red. California fuchsia starts to bloom in late summer and continues through the fall, even into the winter in some coastal locations.

Meadows. Wildflower meadows are becoming increasingly popular alternatives to lawns, and southwestern North American natives such as California poppy, tidy tips, blue-eyed grass, goldfields, showy penstemon, California bluebell, and farewell-to-spring can fill open spaces with color from late winter to early summer. Native wildflower meadows cost less than lawns to maintain, and consume less water, gasoline, fertilizers, and time.

The easiest time to create a wildflower meadow is when the land is bare and you do not have to deal with established, competing grasses, weeds, herbaceous plants, and woody seedlings. Meadow seeds can be purchased from many of the suppliers listed in Appendix A. If you are planning to plant a large area, you should inquire about wholesale prices for wildflower and native grass seed. And if you purchase formulated wildflower-grass seed mixtures, be sure they contain only those native species you really want in your meadow.

Natural valley grasslands and coastal prairies in this region (see page 3) are a combination of wildflowers and grasses. When planning your wildflower meadow select the grasses with great care. The chart below lists native grasses suitable for southwestern meadows. Many of these grasses are "cool-season" grasses that grow in the winter and spring in response to seasonal rains and then dry out and go into dormancy during the summer. The meadow grasses you interplant with the wildflowers should be bunch grasses — species that grow in clumps. Their shoots will provide support and the ideal amount of competition to enable the wildflowers to grow straight and tall. Avoid planting ryegrasses or bluegrasses, which will form a sod turf and crowd out the wildflowers.

Native wildflower seeds should be combined with a mixture of native grasses such as purple needlegrass, blue grama, foothill stipa, and Indian ricegrass, with 60 to 90 percent of the seeds being grasses. The wildflower and grass seed mixture should be sown at a rate of 5 to 20 pounds of live seeds per acre, depending on the species composition. If species with small seeds make up the bulk of the seeds, the seeding rate should be lower than when species with large, heavy seeds are used. The supplier from whom you purchase wildflower and grass seed in bulk can make specific seeding rate recommendations, but typically 6 to 7 pounds of wildflower seeds are mixed with enough grass seeds to sow an acre.

In California it is best to sow the seeds in late autumn before the winter rains. Do not plant the meadow in spring, since the seedlings will not have enough time to become established, or in late summer, when heat and droughty conditions may make it difficult for seeds to germinate and seedlings to become established. In Arizona and New Mexico seeds can be sown in the late spring or early summer before the summer rains begin.

Sow the seeds on a windless day, broadcasting them by hand or using a whirlwind seeder. Keep the soil moist, but not wet, until the seeds have germinated, seedlings start to become established, and the rains have arrived. A light cov-

Native Southwestern Grasses

COMMON NAME	LATIN NAME	HEIGHT	COMMENTS
Sideoats grama	*Bouteloua curtipendula*	24″	Good drought resistance and erosion control; excellent for desert meadows; can be mowed as a lawn.
Blue grama	*Bouteloua gracilis*	15″	Very attractive seed heads.
Tufted hair grass	*Deschampsia caespitosa*	8″	Hardy, lush foliage; mowable as a lawn.
Indian rice-grass	*Oryzopsis hymenoides*	20″	Excellent for meadows or rock gardens; has attractive flowers that can be dried for arrangements; seeds are edible.
Pine bluegrass	*Poa scabrella*	12–30″	Native bunch grass that grows from coast to timberline; summer dormant at low elevations, remains green in mountains.
Purple needlegrass	*Stipa pulchra*	48″	Dried stems golden-yellow; tall bunch grass once the dominant species in CA.
Foothill stipa	*Stipa lepida*	36″	Good for erosion control; delicate flowers; mowable.
Desert stipa	*Stipa speciosa*	24″	Very drought tolerant; blue-green foliage.

Southwestern xeriscape

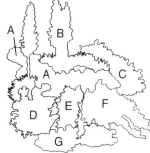

A. Sagebrush
B. Our Lord's candle
C. Ceanothus
D. Prickly poppy
E. Eaton's firecracker
F. California fuchsia
G. Desert marigold

ering of seed-free straw will help to conserve moisture and reduce erosion until the meadow is established. Do not, however, use baled field hay, which is likely to contain the seeds of exotic grasses, species you want to prevent from invading your meadow.

Transforming an Existing Field. More commonly, you are confronted with an existing lawn or field that you want to convert to a wildflower meadow. *Resist the impulse to use herbicides or fumigants to kill the existing vegetation.* Herbicides are likely to create more problems for the wildflower enthusiast than they solve. Apart from the damage they cause to the environment, they are not likely to save you any time in establishing a wildflower meadow. Hand weeding of weeds like black mustard is just as fast as spraying herbicide and much safer.

One way to turn an existing field into a wildflower meadow is to start on a small scale by clearing small patches or strips just before the onset of the rainy

THE WILDFLOWER GARDENER'S GUIDE

season, sowing native annual wildflowers and grasses, and transplanting live perennials later once the rains have arrived, rather than just scattering seeds among established grasses. An even more successful approach for California meadows is to start perennial grass and wildflower plugs (see page 50) during the winter a year ahead and then to prepare the site a spring in advance, before the existing, unwanted field plants produce seeds. In desert areas with summer rains, the timetable should be shifted by six months.

Make patches by turning over sections of the field with a sharp spade or a rototiller. The patches should be 3 to 8 feet in diameter and dug in a random pattern, to create a more natural effect. If you prefer a border effect, clear strips in the field with a rototiller. Remove as many of the existing grass roots as possible, and water the soil to encourage the germination of any weed seeds that you have inadvertently stirred up in the process. Then cover the patch with heavy-gauge black plastic sheet "mulch," pieces of discarded carpet, or even thick sections of newspaper. If you do not care for the sight of such coverings, you can spread a layer of bark mulch or soil on top of them. The covering will eventually shade out and kill off the remaining clumps of grass and the newly germinated weed seedlings.

Remove the coverings in mid-autumn before the rainy season begins. If black plastic mulch or carpet sections have been used, you may be able to use them again. Just place them where you intend to create the next year's patches.

Now plant the grass plugs in the patch, spacing them 12 to 15 inches apart. Transplant perennial native plants in between the clumps of grasses, and sow the seeds of annual wildflowers. The meadow will benefit from watering until the winter rains come, as well as a light mulch of seed-free straw to conserve moisture and reduce erosion.

If your meadow already has bunch grasses, and you do not care to introduce new grass species, wildflower plugs and sods can be planted directly into the field in late autumn. Clear a small patch about a foot in diameter with a cultivator and pick out the grass roots. Set the live plants so the bases of their shoots are at the ground level. Press them down firmly so the roots are in good contact with the soil beneath, and water them.

Wildflower Meadow Maintenance. Repeat the steps each year until you are satisfied with your wildflower and native grass meadow. It may be a slow process, but even in nature a beautiful wildflower meadow, resplendent with a high diversity of desirable plants, is rarely produced in a single year.

Once the wildflower meadow is established it is relatively easy to maintain. Mow the meadow once a year with a rotary mower after the seeds have set. Grasslands are naturally swept by periodic fires. Meadows can be maintained by controlled burning, which kills many invading weed, shrub, and tree seedlings. Do not burn a meadow until after the second season, but then you can burn it every two to three years. Meadows are best burned on windless days, when the dormant grass is dry but the soil is still wet. If the meadow grass is too thin to support the fire, dry straw can be scattered about and ignited. *Be certain to observe local, state, and federal regulations concerning outdoor burning, in addition to the usual safety practices.* Check with your local fire department for assistance in planning any controlled burns and to obtain an outdoor burning permit.

In some suburbs there are ordinances dictating aesthetic standards for landscaping. If you live in such a community you might want to check with your city hall before converting your front yard into a prairie. If there are prohibitions, you can always try to get the law changed to encourage the landscaping use of native plants. Native plants are rarely the "weeds" that these ordinances are trying to prohibit, and it is unlikely that your California poppies or tidy tips are going to march through your neighbor's water-consuming Kentucky bluegrass.

Foothill Woodland Gardens. Foothill woodlands are natural mixtures of grasses and interspersed oaks and other trees. All of the species presented in the grassland section of this book can be grown in the gaps between trees, and some such as Douglas's iris, blue-eyed grass, and western shooting star are even exceptionally well suited to woodland shade. Use care, however, in designing and maintaining plantings under oak trees. Oaks are susceptible to root and crown rots if they receive too much water during the summer. If trees are densely planted or have branches near the ground, companions should be planted at least 6 feet from the trunks to allow proper air circulation. Don't water wildflowers that are directly under tree crowns, since the additional water may encourage tree diseases.

Plant Descriptions

The technical terminology used in the descriptions of the flowers, leaves, shoots, and roots for the species in this book has been kept to a minimum. The knowledge of some botanical terms is essential, however, and relatively painless to acquire.

FLOWERS Illustrated below are two typical flowers with all the parts that are usually present. *Complete flowers* have all the parts illustrated, but some of the wildflowers in the book lack one or more of the parts or they may be fused together in different arrangements. The trillium (below left) is a *simple flower*. The tidy tips (center) is a *composite flower*.

In simple flowers, the flower parts are attached to a fleshy pad (the receptacle) atop the flower stem or *peduncle*. The outermost parts of the flower are the *sepals*, which are usually small, green, leaflike structures that cover and protect the flower while it is in the bud. Collectively, all of the sepals are called the *calyx*, Latin for "cup." In some species the sepals are fused together to form

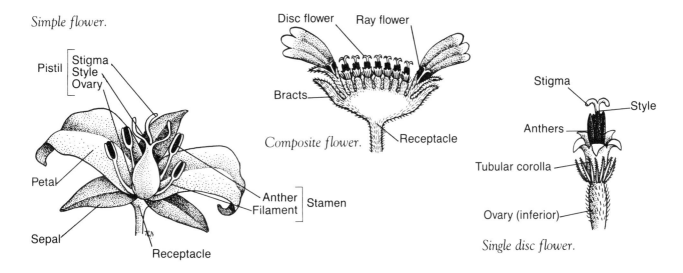

Simple flower.

Pistil [Stigma / Style / Ovary]

Petal

Sepal

Receptacle

Anther / Filament] Stamen

Disc flower   Ray flower

Bracts

Composite flower.   Receptacle

Stigma

Style

Anthers

Tubular corolla

Ovary (inferior)

Single disc flower.

a tubular calyx, and in other species they resemble petals. Immediately inside the sepals are the *petals*, which may take on a variety of forms, some species having petals fused together into a tube, and others having petals that are free and unattached. On some flowers the petal arrangement is radially symmetrical, but on others, the petals take irregular forms. Collectively the petals are called the *corolla*, which means "small crown" in Latin.

In the center of the flower are the sexual parts, the male *stamens* and the female *pistil*. There may be one or several pistils, depending upon the species, but most flowering plants have more than one stamen. The stamen consists of a slender stalk, the *filament*, to which the pollen-bearing sacks, the *anthers*, are attached. The pistil has three major parts whose shapes may vary widely among species. The upper surface of the pistil, which receives pollen grains, is the *stigma*. The stigma is attached to the *ovary* at the base of the pistil by a usually slender tissue known as the *style*. Inside the ovary is a chamber containing the *ovules*, the female sex cells. After the pollen grains are deposited on the stigma, they germinate, sending microscopic tubes down through the style, through portions of the ovary, and finally into the ovules. Following fertilization, the ovules mature into *seeds*, and the ovary matures into the *fruit* of the plant.

The flowers of plants in the aster family, such as desert marigold and tidy tips, have a more complex structure. These species usually have two types of small flowers clustered together in a composite *flower head*. The small flowers or *florets* share a common, broad receptacle which is usually enclosed from below by many leafy bracts. The *ray flowers* usually form a ring around the outside of the head. Each ray flower has a relatively long, straplike petal which upon close inspection can be seen to be several small petals fused together. Often ray flowers are sterile and lack stamens and pistils entirely. In the center of the flower head are the even smaller *disc flowers*, with minute, tubular corollas. The stamens and the pistils in these flowers are surrounded by the petals, but are usually so small that magnification is required to see them clearly.

COLOR AND HEIGHT

Color of the flower and height of the plant are the gardener's first two concerns in deciding what species to plant. To aid in planning, the 34 species of plants described in this book are listed on page 27 by flower color and on page 28 by height. Use the information in these charts as a rough guide only. Keep in mind that some species, such as California poppy, can appear in a range of colors. Also, the height of the plant depends on the environmental conditions in which it is grown. Further information concerning flower color and plant height is given in the descriptions of individual species.

FLOWER COLOR

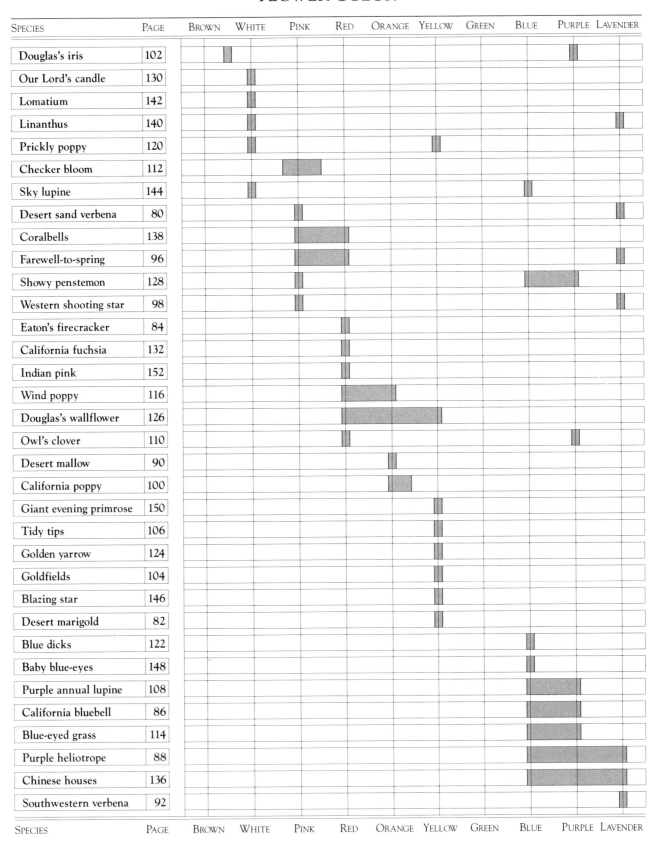

Species	Page	Brown	White	Pink	Red	Orange	Yellow	Green	Blue	Purple	Lavender
Douglas's iris	102		X							X	
Our Lord's candle	130		X								
Lomatium	142		X								
Linanthus	140		X								X
Prickly poppy	120		X				X				
Checker bloom	112			X							
Sky lupine	144		X						X		
Desert sand verbena	80			X							X
Coralbells	138			X	X						
Farewell-to-spring	96			X	X						
Showy penstemon	128			X					X	X	
Western shooting star	98			X							X
Eaton's firecracker	84				X						
California fuchsia	132				X						
Indian pink	152				X						
Wind poppy	116				X	X					
Douglas's wallflower	126				X	X	X				
Owl's clover	110				X					X	
Desert mallow	90					X					
California poppy	100					X	X				
Giant evening primrose	150						X				
Tidy tips	106						X				
Golden yarrow	124						X				
Goldfields	104						X				
Blazing star	146						X				
Desert marigold	82						X				
Blue dicks	122								X		
Baby blue-eyes	148								X		
Purple annual lupine	108								X	X	
California bluebell	86								X	X	
Blue-eyed grass	114								X	X	
Purple heliotrope	88								X	X	X
Chinese houses	136								X	X	
Southwestern verbena	92										X

| Species | Page | Brown | White | Pink | Red | Orange | Yellow | Green | Blue | Purple | Lavender |

PLANT HEIGHT

Species	Page
Desert sand verbena	80
Goldfields	104
California bluebell	86
Blue-eyed grass	114
Owl's clover	110
Linanthus	140
Sky lupine	144
Tidy tips	106
Southwestern verbena	92
Indian pink	152
California fuchsia	132
Lomatium	142
Baby-blue eyes	148
Purple annual lupine	108
Farewell-to-spring	96
Checker bloom	112
Western shooting star	98
Desert marigold	82
Eaton's firecracker	84
Douglas's iris	102
Chinese houses	136
Golden yarrow	124
Wind poppy	116
Coralbells	138
California poppy	100
Douglas's wallflower	126
Purple heliotrope	88
Prickly poppy	120
Blazing star	146
Desert mallow	90
Blue dicks	122
Showy penstemon	128
Giant evening primrose	150
Our Lord's candle	130

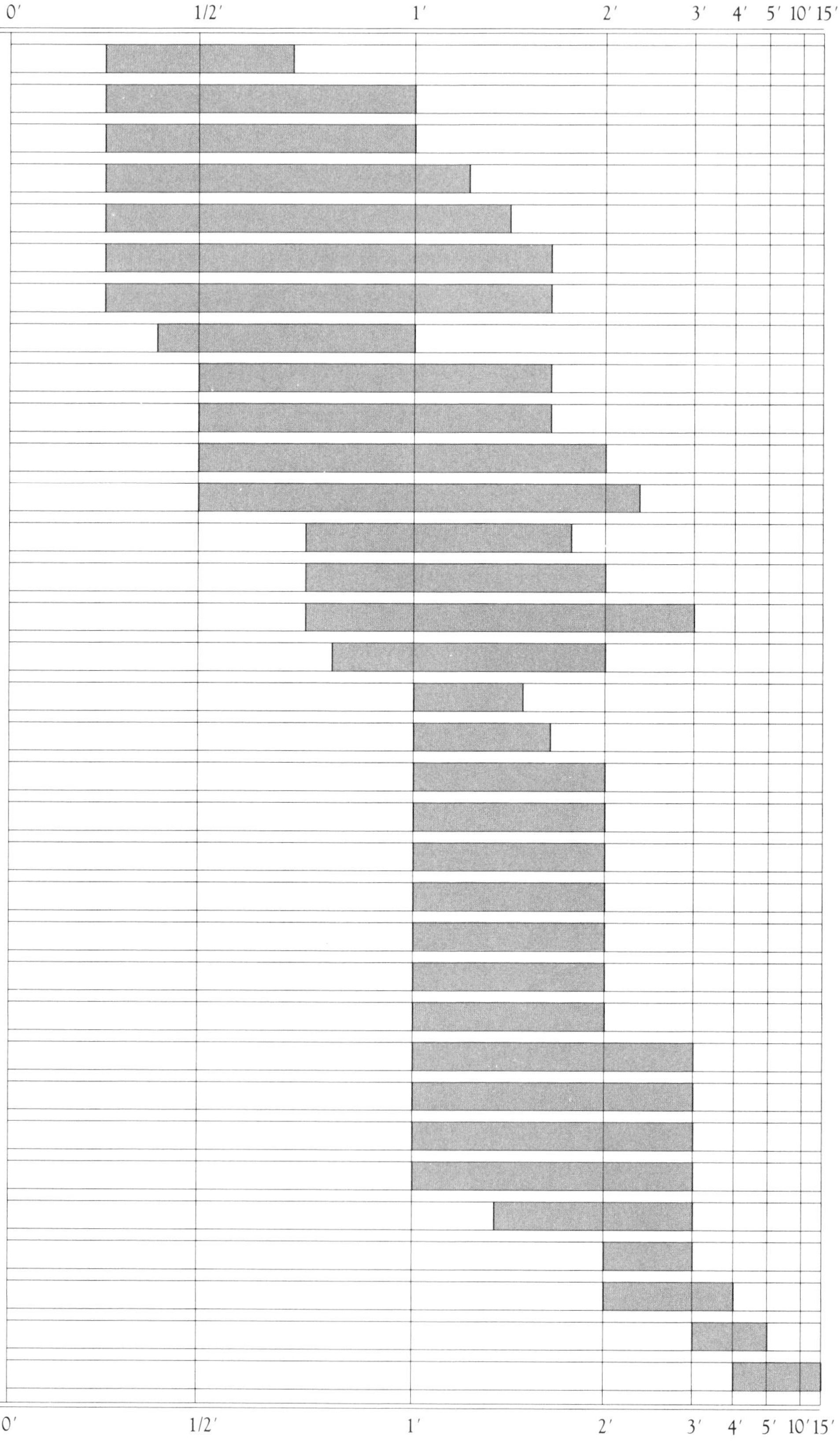

FRUITS AND SEEDS
Fruits are as intriguing and varied as the flowers that produce them. The main function of fruits, which are formed from ripened ovaries, is to aid in the dissemination of the seeds they contain. The structure of various fruits often gives clues about how the seeds are disseminated. Many species that inhabit open spaces, like California fuchsia and desert marigold, depend upon the wind to carry their seeds away from the parent plants and often have small seeds with tufts of hairs to keep them buoyed by air currents. The fruits of desert sand verbena and lomatium are also disseminated by the wind, but along the surface of the ground.

Other wildflowers use different devices to disseminate their seeds through the air. As the long stems of blue dicks wave in the wind, for example, the seeds are flung out of openings in the tops of the capsule fruits. The fruits of the sky lupine, on the other hand, rupture and eject their seeds up to 10 feet away, sometimes making popping sounds as they explode.

ROOT SYSTEMS
The forms of the underground portions of the 34 wildflowers described in this book vary greatly and may influence the types of habitats in which they can be grown. The root system also affects how easily a plant can be propagated. Six of the eight most common "root types" illustrated on pages 29 and 30 are actually the underground stems, or "rootstocks," of perennials. The remaining two are true roots and lack leaf buds.

Runners and Stolons. Underground stems take a variety of forms. The simplest rootstock has thin horizontal branches, which give rise to new plants. These branches are usually called *runners* if they are above ground, as with strawberries, and *stolons* if they are below ground, as with mint.

True Roots. True roots (illustrated on page 30) may be either diffuse and fibrous, as with many garden plants like western shooting star and blue-eyed

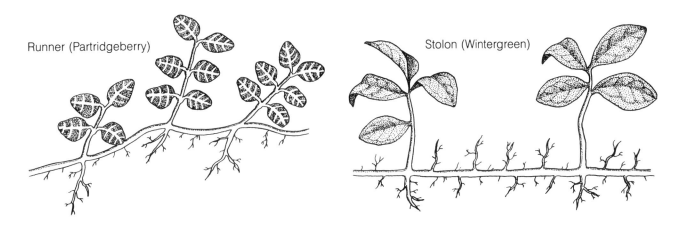

Runner (Partridgeberry)

Stolon (Wintergreen)

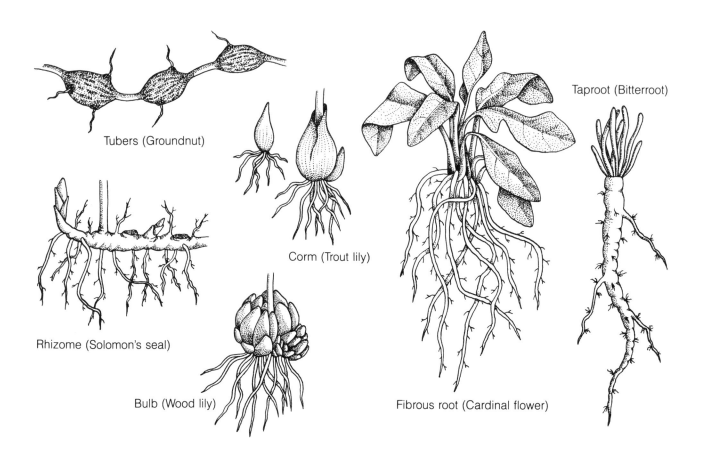

Tubers (Groundnut)

Corm (Trout lily)

Taproot (Bitterroot)

Rhizome (Solomon's seal)

Bulb (Wood lily)

Fibrous root (Cardinal flower)

grass, or they may be a strongly vertical, carrotlike *tap root* as with Indian pink and checker bloom. The root systems of some wildflowers are intermediate between the two basic types.

Tubers. If the tip of a stolon produces a swollen, fleshy storage organ, it is called a *tuber*. The leaf buds of tubers are frequently called "eyes." The potato is probably the most familiar example of a tuber, but wildflowers such as lomatium also have tuberous roots.

Rhizomes. Thick, fleshy, horizontal, underground stems with buds on their top surfaces and roots on their bottom surfaces are called *rhizomes*. Rhizomes, like those of Douglas's iris and coralbells, store large amounts of starch, which is used to nourish the shoots and flowers of perennials as they emerge from dormancy.

Corms and Bulbs. Rootstocks may also be round and bulbous. A true *bulb* is a bud atop a very short stem, surrounded by fleshy leaf scales, as with onions and tulips. *Corms* look like bulbs but are rootstocks formed from the swollen, solid base of the stem, as with gladiolus and blue dicks.

Flowering Season

A great number of factors, some genetic and some environmental, affect the onset and length of the flowering season of wildflowers. Complex interactions among climatic factors such as amount of sunlight, length of day, moisture, and temperature of air and soil influence exactly when plants start flowering.

Annual species usually have longer flowering seasons than perennials do and, of course, flower in a single growing season. Annuals may become persistent, even to the point of being considered weeds, through self-seeding. Perennials, on the other hand, may require several or many years to reach maturity and flower, but once established they generally require little maintenance, and reliably reappear year after year.

CLIMATE   The overall climatic patterns of temperature and precipitation have a considerable effect on the blooming of wildflowers. In general, coastal areas, with the moderating effects of the Pacific Ocean, have more constant temperatures and longer growing seasons than do inland sites. They also tend to have more reliable precipitation than inland sites do, although rainfall is highly variable everywhere in the Southwest.

Precipitation and temperature are critical, influencing the timing of germination, the renewal of perennial growth, and the abundance of wildflowers. In years when the winter rains are erratic or far below average, especially if it is also unusually cold, springtime flowering of annuals may be minimal. On the other hand, if the rainy season precipitation is well distributed and slightly above average, wildflowers may germinate and flower abundantly.

The timing of precipitation is especially important for desert annuals. Some, like desert sand verbena, respond to the warm summer rains and are known as "summer annuals." Others, "winter annuals" like phacelias, germinate in response to cooler winter rains.

Even though exact flowering times frequently vary, the flowering order of wildflower species within the same geographic area tends to be consistent from year to year. The general seasonal progression of flowering of the wildflowers in this book is shown on page 32. The seasons of flowering are given, rather

FLOWERING PROGRESSION

Species	Page	Late Winter	Early Spring	Midspring	Late Spring	Early Summer	Summer	Late Summer	Early Fall	Fall
Blue-eyed grass	114	■	■							
Checker bloom	112	■	■	■						
Giant evening primrose	150	■	■	■			■	■	■	
California bluebell	86	■	■	■	■	■				
Desert sand verbena	80	■	■	■	■	■				
California poppy	100	■	■	■	■	■	■	■	■	
Lomatium	142		■	■	■					
Eaton's firecracker	84		■	■	■	■	■			
Baby blue-eyes	148		■	■						
Western shooting star	98		■							
Douglas's wallflower	126		■	■						
Golden yarrow	124		■	■	■	■	■			
Southwestern verbena	92			■	■	■	■	■		
Owl's clover	110			■						
Blue dicks	122			■						
Desert mallow	90			■						
Goldfields	104			■						
Blazing star	146			■						
Purple annual lupine	108			■						
Wind poppy	116			■						
Our Lord's candle	130				■					
Showy penstemon	128				■					
Chinese houses	136				■	■				
Tidy tips	106				■	■				
Sky lupine	144				■	■				
Purple heliotrope	88				■	■	■			
Linanthus	140				■	■	■			
Indian pink	152				■	■	■			
Desert marigold	82				■	■	■	■	■	
Farewell-to-spring	96				■	■	■			
Prickly poppy	120					■	■	■		
Coralbells	138					■	■	■		
California fuchsia	132							■	■	■

than calendar months, because the onset of the growing season varies from locale to locale and from year to year. The seasons refer to the flowering of a given species near the center of its native range, and the gardener may find that the flowering sequence may be slightly different for plants obtained from different areas.

LOCAL CONDITIONS

The exact time of flowering in your garden may also be influenced by local conditions such as slope, elevation, soil type, and mulches. If your garden slopes to the south, it will be warmer and spring will arrive sooner than if it slopes to the north. The warmest slopes are those on which the sun's rays strike most perpendicularly, but even a 5-degree south-facing slope may have a microclimate equivalent to that of a flat surface 300 miles farther south. A similar slope facing north would be correspondingly cooler. A garden located at the base of a mountain or a hill, on the other hand, may be chilled by the downslope settling of cold air, especially in the spring and fall. Flowering dates may vary by as much as several weeks, therefore, depending on the local topography.

The elevation of a garden will also influence how rapidly spring arrives. At a given latitude air temperatures generally decrease 3 degrees F per 1,000 feet of rise. For each 100-foot increase in elevation, the air temperature is only three-tenths of a degree cooler, but flowering is delayed by about one day. For example, it is possible in June to drive from Lone Pine (elevation 3,700 feet) in the Owens Valley of California to Whitney Portal (elevation 8,400 feet), and go in 10 miles from baking desert to fields of snow.

Proximity to the ocean, especially during the late spring and early summer fog season, may influence how rapidly plants grow and flower. It is not uncommon for coastal sites enshrouded in fog to be 20 degrees F or more cooler than areas several miles away. Onshore winds will also tend to reduce air temperatures during the spring and summer.

Soil conditions may advance or retard the progression of flowering. Sandy soils generally warm up more rapidly in the spring than do peaty or clayey soils. Dark-colored soils will warm more rapidly than light-colored soils will. Heavy mulches, while reducing frost and keeping soils warmer in the winter, provide an insulation layer that may both slow the warming in the spring and maintain cooler soils in the summer.

GENETIC FACTORS

Some plants, but not all, are genetically programmed to flower in response to specific day lengths or hours of darkness. This characteristic is found in a wide variety of wildflowers, including annuals, biennials, and perennials. Some plants, such as California poppy, grow vegetatively in the winter when the days are short and then flower most abundantly when days lengthen and nights become short. They are known as "long-day" plants, although they are actually responding to the short nights associated with late spring and early summer. The northern regions of North America, with relatively longer spring and summer day lengths, have a greater proportion of long-day plants than do southern regions. In fact, day length determines the southern limits of some long-day species.

Other species, such as the California fuchsia, are "short-day" plants and flower when days are short and nights are long. These species are stimulated to flower by the long nights of late summer and fall.

Regional differences in climatic patterns and day lengths have led to the evolution of genetically distinct varieties in some wildflower species. Known as "ecotypes," these varieties are well adapted to local conditions. When individuals of different ecotypes are planted together in the same garden, they frequently will flower at different times.

EXTENDING THE FLOWERING SEASON

There are several ways in which the flowering season can be prolonged. The easiest way to extend the flower season of annual wildflowers is to make successive plantings at three-to-four-week intervals from the beginning of the rainy season to late winter. Some of the late sowings may not bear flowers, but there will still be blooms after the flowers of the first sowing have long withered. Some wildflowers will bloom longer if additional water is provided during the dry season, while others will simply rot. Consult the cultural requirements for individual wildflowers presented in Part III.

With some species, such as Douglas's wallflower, trim some of the plants just before they set flower buds. That will delay their flowering by several weeks, and the clipped plants will come into bloom as the flowers on the untrimmed plants are fading. Desert marigolds grown from seeds will tend to flower later the first year than in subsequent years. By planting new seeds just before the onset of the rainy season each year, you can have flowers well into the autumn. Many species, both annuals and perennials, will bloom longer if the fading flowers are removed ("deadheaded") before the fruits and seeds start to mature. The only drawback of this technique is that you sacrifice production of seed that could be used for further propagation.

If you have a number of different garden sites with varying slopes and exposures, the differences in microclimates may be sufficient to accelerate flowering in some plants and delay it in others. Another way to extend the flowering season of a given species is to purchase seeds or plants from suppliers in various geographic regions, so that different ecotypes are represented in the garden. The differences in their flowering times may be sufficient to prolong the season even of those species with short-lived flowers.

Wildflower Culture

LIGHT
CONDITIONS

While the vast majority of domesticated horticultural species planted in the garden require full sunlight for optimum growth, native plants have evolved to survive in a wide variety of light conditions, from full sun to shade. Therein lies an opportunity in gardening with wildflowers. The light preferences of the 34 species of native plants included in this book are given on page 36.

While some species are successfully grown only in a rather restricted range of light conditions, others can be cultivated in either sun or shade. The form of the plant often changes when grown under different light conditions. Typically when a plant is grown in the shade its leaves are thinner and larger and its stems are more spindly or "leggy" than when it is grown in the open. Some species, such as baby blue-eyes and Chinese houses, are so adapted to shade that they suffer leaf scorching if they have prolonged exposure to full sun on dry sites. Coralbells can withstand even deeper shade, but can be grown in full sun if sufficient water is provided.

TEMPERATURE

Most gardeners are familiar with hardiness zones, which indicate the relative mildness or severity of winter temperatures. (See page 58, U.S.D.A. Hardiness Zone Map.) The higher the hardiness zone number, the milder the winter climate. There is a great deal of similarity between hardiness zones and the length of the frost-free season (see map on page 57). Hardiness zones are based only on the average annual minimum winter temperature, however, and the frost-free season is the average length of time between the last killing frost in the spring and the first frost in the autumn. As you move from southern coastal to northern interior regions of southwestern North America, you will generally encounter shorter frost-free seasons and lower hardiness zone numbers, but this pattern is by no means uniform. The Pacific Coast has a significantly milder winter and a longer growing season than do the peaks of the Coast Ranges, the Sierra Nevada, and the high-elevation inland plateaus at the same latitude.

Most perennials have a limited range of hardiness zones in which they can survive. The approximate range of hardiness zones for the species of wildflow-

LIGHT CONDITIONS

Species	Page	Open Full Sun	Filtered Sun Partial Shade	Light Shade	Heavy Shade
Blazing star	146	▓			
Blue dicks	122	▓			
Blue-eyed grass	114	▓			
California bluebells	86	▓			
California poppy	100	▓			
Desert mallow	90	▓			
Desert marigold	82	▓			
Desert sand verbena	80	▓			
Douglas's wallflower	126	▓			
Eaton's firecracker	84	▓			
Giant evening primrose	150	▓			
Golden yarrow	124	▓			
Linanthus	140	▓			
Our Lord's candle	130	▓			
Owl's clover	110	▓			
Prickly poppy	120	▓			
Purple heliotrope	88	▓			
Purple annual lupine	108	▓			
Showy penstemon	128	▓			
Sky lupine	144	▓			
Southwestern verbena	92	▓			
Tidy tips	106	▓			
California fuchsia	132	▓▓			
Goldfields	104	▓▓			
Checker bloom	112	▓▓▓			
Indian pink	152	▓▓▓			
Lomatium	142	▓▓▓			
Farewell-to-spring	96	▓▓▓			
Baby blue-eyes	148	▓▓▓	▓		
Wind poppy	116	▓▓▓	▓▓		
Chinese houses	136	▓▓▓	▓▓▓		
Western shooting star	98	▓▓▓	▓▓▓	▓	
Coralbells	138	▓▓▓	▓▓▓	▓▓	
Douglas's iris	102	▓▓▓	▓▓▓	▓▓	

ers in this book is given on page 38 and is shown on the individual range maps. The hardiness ranges indicated are approximate. You can usually cultivate perennials in colder areas if you insulate them with a heavy overwinter mulch to prevent frost penetration in the soil. Be careful to remove the mulch in the spring and to choose a mulching material that will not alter the desired acidity/alkalinity conditions for pH-sensitive species, as is explained in the section to follow concerning soils. Some short-lived or tender perennials like California poppy can be grown as annuals if mulching is not practical.

Many plants need chilling of their seeds as well. These seeds require or are enhanced by weeks or even months of exposure to temperatures of 40 degrees F or below, to break their dormancy and germinate properly, as is discussed in the following section on propagation.

MOISTURE CONDITIONS

Just as wildflowers of the region have adapted to different temperature and light conditions, they have evolved to survive under different moisture conditions, ranging from the deserts of Death Valley to the vernal pools and tule wetlands of grasslands. Rain in southwestern North America is generally abundant during the wet season and scanty during the dry season, but its geographic distribution is far from uniform. Although precipitation generally decreases from the Coast to interior deserts, the maximum precipitation is found near the summits of the mountain ranges. These ranges trap moisture-laden air as it travels inland, creating arid conditions on their eastern slopes. The Central Valley grassland is in the "rain shadow" of the Coast Ranges, and the Great Basin deserts are in the rain shadow of the Cascades and Sierra Nevada Ranges (see the map on page 56).

On a local scale, the gardener should choose wildflowers adapted to the soil-moisture conditions that are present, as shown in the chart on page 40. Some species, such as Douglas's iris and coralbells, thrive in wet soils, yet can also be easily cultivated in well-drained soils of moderate moisture — conditions typical of most flower gardens. Many species need moisture while they are becoming established in the garden, but then they grow better if the soils are not overly wet. Wildflower gardeners should be judicious with the hose; desert marigold, penstemons, and other species suffer from root rot if the soil is too wet, and seedlings of most wildflowers are especially sensitive to fungal attack when soils are cold and wet.

Cultivating wildflowers is easiest when you match a species' optimal requirements with those naturally occurring in the garden, so consider your soil before selecting the wildflowers. If your soil is sandy, it will probably drain quickly, and you should consider planting species that do well in drier conditions. Clayey and peaty soils are often poorly drained, making them hospitable to species

HARDINESS ZONES

Species		Page	1	2	3	4	5	6	7	8	9	10
Desert mallow		90				■	■	■	■			
Coralbells		138				■	■	■	■	■		
Eaton's firecracker		84				■	■	■	■	■	■	■
Giant evening primrose		150				■	■	■	■	■	■	■
Douglas's wallflower		126						■	■	■	■	■
California poppy		100							■	■	■	■
Desert marigold		82							■	■	■	■
Southwestern verbena		92							■	■		
Indian pink		152								■	■	
Golden yarrow		124								■	■	
Western shooting star		98								■	■	
Blue dicks		122									■	
Blue-eyed grass		114									■	
California fuchsia		132									■	
Checker bloom		112									■	
Douglas's iris		102									■	
Lomatium		142									■	
Our Lord's candle		130									■	
Showy penstemon		128									■	
Baby blue-eyes	HA	148										
Blazing star	HA	146										
California bluebell	HA	86										
Chinese houses	HA	136										
Desert sand verbena	SA	80										
Farewell-to-spring	HA	96										
Goldfields	SA	104										
Linanthus	TA	140										
Owl's clover	HA	110										
Prickly poppy	TA	120										
Purple annual lupine	HA	108										
Purple heliotrope	HA	88										
Sky lupine	HA	144										
Tidy tips	HA	106										
Wind poppy	HA	116										

Species	Page	1	2	3	4	5	6	7	8	9	10

HA (Hardy Annual): Seeds can withstand cold winter temperatures.
SA (Semi-hardy Annual): Seeds can withstand cool winter temperatures.
TA (Tender Annual): Limited to areas with mild winters.

preferring plenty of soil moisture during the rainy season, but they can become excessively dry during the remainder of the year.

If your soil conditions do not quite suit a particular species, however, you may be able to add the proper soil amendments before planting. A little extra time and energy invested in site preparation will pay large dividends in the future, so do not rush your wildflowers into soils to which they are ill adapted. Avoid merely piling soil amendments on top of the soil where they will have marginal effect; instead, work them thoroughly into the soil. Organic matter well mixed into the soil will aerate it and increase its water-holding capacity.

If your soil is too dry, the garden not too large, and your hose long enough, it is obviously easy to increase the soil moisture by watering. However, adding clay, compost, humus, or even coarse organic matter such as leaves may be a more effective way of assuring the long-term retention of moisture. Mulches are an integral part of xeriscaping because they reduce evaporation from the soil surface. They are excellent to use around the bases of perennials, but may prevent small seeded annual wildflowers from self-seeding.

If the soil is too wet during the rainy season because of an overabundance of clay, you can improve the drainage by adding sand or gravel mixed with copious amounts of compost or other organic matter. The organic matter creates additional air spaces in clayey soil and helps to prevent the clay from merely coating the grains of sand. Alternatively, gypsum (calcium sulfate) can be added to clayey soil to improve drainage. Since gypsum is an acidifying agent, it should be used where you will be planting wildflowers that thrive in acid soil, with a pH of 5.5 and below. Gypsum has the additional benefit of helping conserve nitrogen compounds in the soil. It is available at many garden or building-supply centers.

pH, SALINITY, AND OTHER SOIL CONDITIONS
The specific soil requirements of 34 native plants are given on the individual species description pages. Some species thrive where nutrient levels are high and humus is abundant in the soil. Other species do best where there is little organic matter and the soil fertility is low.

One of the most important conditions in the cultivation of many wildflowers is the pH of the soil. The pH is simply a measure of the relative acidity or alkalinity on a scale from 0 (most acidic) to 14 (most alkaline), with a value of 7 indicating neutral conditions. The pH units are based on multiples of ten, so that a soil with a pH of 4.0 is 10 times more acidic than a soil with a pH of 5.0, and 100 times more acidic than a soil with a pH of 6.0. Likewise, a pH of 9 is 10 times more alkaline than a pH of 8, and so forth.

The pH of the soil is important because it influences the availability of nutrients essential for plant growth. Nutrients such as phosphorus, calcium, potas-

SOIL MOISTURE CONDITIONS

Species	Page	Wet	Damp	Moist	Moderately or Seasonally Dry	Arid
Blue-eyed grass	114	●	●	●		
Baby blue-eyes	148		●			
Douglas's iris	102		●	●		
Giant evening primrose	150		●	●		
Goldfields	104		●	●		
Checker bloom	112		●	●	●	
Wind poppy	116		●	●	●	●
Chinese houses	136			●		
Lomatium	142			●	●	
Tidy tips	106			●	●	
Coralbells	138			●	●	
California poppy	100			●	●	●
Western shooting star	98			●		
Farewell-to-spring	96			●		
Blazing star	146			●		
Showy penstemon	128			●		
Purple heliotrope	88			●	●	
Douglas's wallflower	126			●	●	
Linanthus	140			●	●	
Owl's clover	110			●	●	●
Southwestern verbena	92			●	●	●
Our Lord's candle	130				●	
Sky lupine	144				●	
Golden yarrow	124				●	
Purple annual lupine	108				●	
Prickly poppy	120				●	
Indian pink	152				●	
Blue dicks	122				●	
Desert mallow	90				●	●
Desert sand verbena	80				●	●
California bluebell	86				●	●
Eaton's firecracker	84				●	●
California fuchsia	132				●	●
Desert marigold	82					●

| Species | Page | Wet | Damp | Moist | Moderately or Seasonally dry | Arid |

40

sium, and magnesium are most available to plants when the soil pH is between 6.0 and 7.5. Under highly acidic (low pH) conditions these nutrients become insoluble and relatively unavailable for uptake by plants. However, iron, trace minerals, and some toxic elements such as aluminum become more available at low pH. A major concern about acid rain is the possible increased absorption of these toxic elements by plants.

High soil pH may also decrease the availability of nutrients. If the soil is more alkaline than pH 8, phosphorus, iron, and many trace minerals become insoluble and unavailable for plant uptake.

The availability of nitrogen, one of plants' three key nutrients, is influenced by pH conditions as well. Much of the nitrogen that plants eventually use is bound within organic matter, and the conversion of this bound nitrogen to forms available to plants is accomplished by several species of bacteria living in the soil. When the soil's pH drops below 5.5, the activity of these bacteria is inhibited, and little nitrogen is available to the plants.

The usual pH range of soils is from about 4 to about 8. Over millennia, rocks and minerals decompose and slowly release large amounts of potassium, calcium, magnesium, and other alkaline nutrients. In humid areas of North America ample rainfall has removed these elements from the soil. In much of the arid Southwest, however, intense evaporation and scanty rainfall have led to accumulation of these constituents and the production of highly alkaline or saline soils in many locations. As a result the soils of the region tend to range from only slightly acidic to highly alkaline, with pH values substantially above 7. Poorly designed or operated irrigation systems further contribute to increased salinity in the Southwest by bringing additional salts to the soil surface. In some low-lying basins salt deposits even encrust the surface of the soil, making the growth of most plants impossible.

Local soil acidity/alkalinity conditions may also vary because of differences in bedrock geology or vegetation. In general, limestone or marble bedrock produces mildly alkaline soils, and granite bedrock produces acidic soils.

Along the Coast Ranges there are frequent outcrops of the lustrous gray-green mineral serpentine. Many species of domesticated and native plants grow very poorly, if at all, in serpentine areas, because the soil is deficient in calcium yet has an overabundance of magnesium and toxic metals such as nickel and cadmium. Heavy applications of ground limestone can overcome the lack of calcium and reduce the toxicity of metals in these soils.

Certain species of plants may also increase the acidity of the soil through the addition of organic matter with a low pH. Coniferous forests are noted for their acidic soils. The dead foliage of pines, spruce, fir, as well as oaks and heath plants, deposited on top of the soil, further acidifies the soil as it decomposes.

In cool, wet areas, the growth of mosses may also create locally the acidic conditions typical of regions with needle-leaved forests.

Some species of wildflowers are relatively insensitive to soil acidity/alkalinity conditions, while others survive only over a narrow pH range. Most often pH preferences are more related to the balance of various nutrients required by particular species, or to changes in the biological activity of soil organisms, rather than to acidity or alkalinity itself. On page 43 is a guide to the pH preferences of those species of wildflowers that have specific soil pH requirements. It is often difficult to grow species close together if they have vastly different pH requirements. It is best to grow acid-loving species, such as Indian pink, in a different section of the garden than species that prefer alkaline soils.

HOW TO MEASURE pH

Before deciding which wildflowers to cultivate and where to plant them, it is essential to know something about the pH of your soils. The measurement is actually quite simple, and there are a number of commercial products readily available from most garden suppliers. The pH is measured by taking samples of soil from the root zone at several different spots in the garden. Using a plastic spoon, place the soil in a small plastic or glass vial, and add an equal volume of water. Shake or stir the sample to mix the soil and water thoroughly, and allow the soil to settle. The pH of the liquid in the top of the vial can then be determined by any one of several means.

The least expensive way to measure pH is with "indicator paper," which can be purchased in short strips or long rolls. This is like litmus paper, but rather than merely showing you whether a solution is acid or alkaline, it produces a range of colors to indicate the pH value. Just stick the strip of paper into the liquid extracted from the soil and compare the color of the dampened paper to the reference chart provided.

A slightly more accurate method, although usually more expensive, is the use of indicator solutions, which are frequently sold in pH kits. A small amount of the liquid extracted from the soil-and-water mix is placed in a ceramic dish, and a few drops of indicator solution are added. As with the indicator papers, the color produced is compared to a pH reference chart.

You can also measure pH with a meter. One type of pH meter operates without batteries and measures pH based on the conductivity of the moistened soil. This type of pH meter is neither more accurate nor faster than the color-indicator methods that use solutions or paper. All provide a rough, but useful, estimate of soil pH.

The most accurate measurements of soil pH use electronic meters with one or several electrodes. These instruments are quite expensive and are used by

pH PREFERENCES

Species	Page	3	4	5	6	7	8	9	10
Indian pink	152								
Coralbells	138								
Western shooting star	98								
Baby-blue eyes	148								
Blazing star	146								
Blue dicks	122								
Blue-eyed grass	114								
California bluebell	86								
California fuchsia	132								
California poppy	100								
Checker bloom	112								
Chinese houses	136								
Desert mallow	90								
Desert marigold	82								
Desert sand verbena	80								
Douglas's iris	102								
Douglas's wallflower	126								
Eaton's firecracker	84								
Giant evening primrose	150								
Golden yarrow*	124								
Goldfields	104								
Linanthus	140								
Lomatium	142								
Our Lord's candle	130								
Owl's clover	110								
Prickly poppy	120								
Purple annual lupine	108								
Purple heliotrope	88								
Sky lupine	144								
Showy penstemon	128								
Southwestern verbena	92								
Tidy tips	106								
Wind poppy	116								

*This and the following species appear to have no strong pH preferences.

Species	Page	3	4	5	6	7	8	9	10

soil-testing laboratories for determining soil pH. Most state Agricultural Experiment Stations, usually located at land-grant universities, will test soil samples for a nominal charge. To arrange for such pH testing, contact your state's land-grant university or your county's Agricultural Extension Service agent.

CHANGING THE pH OF SOILS

You may find that the pH of your soil does not suit a particular species, even though all other environmental conditions seem perfect. The acidity or alkalinity of soils can be altered to a limited extent through the addition of various soil amendments. It may take several years to change a soil's pH permanently, however, so be patient.

Pine, spruce, and fir needles can be added to garden soils to lower the pH. If none of these is locally available, peat moss also works well in acidifying soils. Powdered gypsum (calcium sulfate) or sulfur powder can be used to lower soil pH, but these should be used with caution, because they act more rapidly than the organic materials.

Ground limestone is the amendment of choice to raise the pH of the soil. Medium-ground limestone may give better long-term results than very coarse limestone (which may be slow to neutralize soil acids) or very fine limestone (which may be lost too quickly from the soil). Wood ashes can also be used, but keep in mind that they are more concentrated than limestone and may even "burn" wildflowers if too much is applied.

After measuring the pH, add the soil amendment, taking care to mix thoroughly and incorporate it uniformly in the top 6 to 12 inches of soil. Spread the amendment thinly on the ground, and work it into the soil with a spading fork or shovel. Then add another layer, mixing it into the soil. If you do not mix the amendment evenly you may find pockets of soil with enormously different pH values. Moisten the soil, and then allow it to rest for a day or so before again measuring the pH at several spots. Repeat the process until you have the desired pH conditions.

A very rough rule of thumb is that for a 100-square-foot area of most soils it takes about 2 to 6 pounds of limestone to raise the pH one unit, and 2½ to 7 pounds of gypsum or ½ to 2 pounds of sulfur to lower the pH one unit. Clay soils require more of an amendment to change the pH; sandy soils, less.

It is strongly recommended that organic matter acidifiers be used before resorting to gypsum or sulfur. It is better to change the pH of the soil slowly than to overdo it one way and then the other.

After the appropriate pH is attained, check it periodically. Since the natural processes at work in your garden will be altering the pH through rainfall, bacterial activity, the uptake of nutrients by plants, and climatic factors, you may occasionally have to make further additions of soil amendments. With wildflowers in place, be especially careful to add the amendments in small amounts directly on the surface of the soil, and work them in with minimal disturbance of the plants' roots.

A WORD ABOUT WEEDS AND PESTS

Wildflowers growing in their natural habitats are obviously well adapted for survival under the prevailing local conditions. Gardening, however, involves disturbing the soil and modifying the moisture and, often, light conditions. These changes often invite unwelcome and unwanted plants — weeds.

Many of the worst weeds, such as yellow oxalis, spotted spurge, erodium, and yellow mustard, have their origins in the Mediterranean region and have found a new home to their liking in the Southwest. In contrast to many of the desirable native wildflowers, weeds tend to grow quickly, spread aggressively, and set loose copious quantities of highly mobile seeds. Often weeds will accomplish these feats so quickly that they produce many generations in the time it takes to produce a single generation of desired wildflowers. The seeds of weeds tend to be long-lived and may remain dormant for many years, buried in the soil, just waiting for the proper conditions to germinate. Studies have shown that the seeds of some weeds can remain dormant yet capable of germinating for more than forty years. Typically, there are hundreds of weed seeds beneath each square yard of soil surface. Gardening activity frequently brings the weed seeds to the surface and provides ideal conditions for them to thrive.

Weeds are thus inevitable, but do not despair, and *do not resort to the use of herbicides!* Many wildflowers are particularly sensitive to the effects of herbicides, so weeding by hand is the only real choice. You will find that a modest investment of time spent weeding while your wildflowers are first becoming established will pay large dividends. Even natural gardens may need some weeding during the first several years. Once the plants are well established and holding their ground, weeds will have a more difficult time invading, and weeding will be less necessary.

You will find from time to time that various insects will visit your wildflowers, and while some of these may be there for an attractive meal, they usually have an abundance of natural predators that will keep their populations in check so that minimal damage occurs. Some wildflowers, like lupines, may look a bit tattered by the end of the season, because butterfly larvae have chewed holes in the leaves. Usually the plants have suffered little, and *the use of pesticides is unwarranted*, especially if you are trying to attract butterflies or even hummingbirds to the garden. The use of pesticides is also to be avoided because many wildflowers are pollinated by insects, and without the pollinators, there is no fruit and seed production.

When establishing or maintaining a wildflower garden, slugs, household pets, ground squirrels, and, in rural areas, deer may be more of a problem than insects are. If dogs, cats, or deer become a nuisance, fencing may be the only reasonable solution.

Slugs and snails relish certain species of wildflowers, especially those in the lily family. They feed at night when the humidity is high, and can do considerable damage by chewing and stripping leaves. Slugs and snails can be easily and effectively controlled by hand picking, or if you find that approach offensive, by setting out dishes filled with stale beer. The shallow tubs in which whipped cream cheese or margarine are packaged make ideal traps. Fill the tubs three-quarters full with beer and set them about the garden. The snails and slugs much prefer beer to your wildflowers, and once swimming in the brew they drown. Every several days, especially after heavy rains, you may have to dispose of the contents and replenish the beer.

Wildflower Propagation

One of the pleasures of growing wildflowers is the opportunity to propagate them and thereby increase their numbers in your garden. As already pointed out, digging wildflowers from their native environments is not only unethical, but also frequently illegal. The best way to obtain wildflowers for your garden is to purchase seeds, plants or planting stock from reputable suppliers who sell nursery-propagated material (see Appendix A). Once these wildflowers are established, they can serve as stock for further propagation.

SEEDS Seeds are by far the cheapest way to propagate large numbers of wildflowers, even though some perennials grown from seeds may take a long time before they are mature enough to flower. Usually seeds are collected when the fruits are mature. Many species have seed dispersal mechanisms which may make it difficult to find plants with the fruits present when you want to harvest them. One way to capture the seeds before they are released from the plant is to cut a foot-long section of a discarded nylon stocking and make a sleeve, tying off one end with a string or twisted wire closure. Slip the sleeve over the developing fruit after the flower petals have withered, but before the fruit is fully ripe. Firmly but gently tie the open end closed so that the seeds can't fall to the ground, being careful not to crush or break the stem in the process. When the fruits are fully ripe, snip the stem just below the nylon bag, put it in a labeled paper sack, and bring it indoors for further processing.

Some seeds should be planted fresh and not allowed to dry out, or germination will be delayed. Other seeds will not germinate immediately and have to undergo a process of "after-ripening" before they are ready to sprout. Seeds of fleshy fruits should generally be separated from the pulp prior to storage or planting. If seeds are not the kind that need to be planted immediately and you desire to store them for a while, allow them to air-dry for several weeks and then separate the seeds from the dried remains of the fruit. Gently crushing the dried fruits on a large sheet of white paper will usually release the seeds, which should then be separated from the chaff. The chaff can be removed either by blowing gently across the paper or, if seeds are small enough, by sifting through a strainer. Store the cleaned seeds in small manila coin envelopes, zip-closure bags, or 35mm film canisters.

The seeds of some species will remain dormant unless they undergo certain specific treatments — chilling, scratching of their seed coats, exposure to light or darkness, heating by fire, or a combination of these treatments. The treatments required to germinate specific seeds are detailed on the descriptive pages following this chapter. These treatments fall into four catagories: 1) seed chilling, or *stratification*, 2) seed-coat scratching, or *scarification*, 3) heat treatments, 4) light or dark treatment.

Stratification. Some plants that live in southwestern North America have evolved seeds that are dormant the first fall after they have been produced. This adaptation prevents tender seedlings from coming up and facing freezing temperatures when they would be only a month or so old. Breaking dormancy requires the seeds to be subjected to a period of cold temperatures (stratification), followed by a period of warm temperatures — as in the natural progression of seasons. Usually a temperature of only 40 degrees F is sufficient to break dormancy or enhance germination. The length of stratification varies widely among different species. Some seeds germinate more successfully if they are stratified under moist conditions in addition to the cold temperatures.

The easiest way to stratify seeds in the Southwest is to plant the seeds outdoors in the fall and let Nature do it for you. Seeds can be planted directly in the garden where desired or in flats that are left outdoors. If you do not desire to plant the seeds in the fall, place the container or envelope of seeds under refrigeration for the appropriate period of time. If moist stratification is required, the seeds can be placed in damp sphagnum moss or rolled up in lightly dampened paper towels and placed in an air-tight container or zip-closure plastic bag for the duration of the stratification.

Scarification. In order for seeds to germinate they have to take up water and oxygen from the outside environment through the outer covering of the seed, called the *seed coat*. Some native species, especially those in the bean family, have seed coats so tough that water and oxygen cannot enter. These seeds remain dormant until the seed coat is scratched, or scarified. This occurs naturally when seeds are moved around in the soil, especially following heavy rainstorms, but in the home garden better results are obtained if the seeds are scarified by the gardener before planting.

The easiest way to scarify medium-size seeds is to rub the seeds between two sheets of medium-grit sandpaper. You don't want to rub them so hard that you pulverize the seeds, just hard enough to scratch up the surface so that moisture can penetrate to the seed inside. Large seeds can be scarified by nicking the seed coat with a sharp pocket knife.

Heat Treatments. The seeds of many of the chaparral plants are adapted to germinate following fire, and some will remain dormant until heated. In addition, inhibitors that prevent germination in some of these wildflowers appear to be removed by *charate*, the charred remains of burned chaparral plants. The easiest way to simulate the scorching of a chaparral fire is to fill a clay flower pot (the plastic ones will melt) with sand, sprinkle the seeds to be treated on the surface, and cover with a ¼–½-inch-thick layer of pine needles. In a safe place, ignite the pine needles and allow them to burn until extinguished. When the surface of the pot has cooled, gently scoop out the seeds and charate with a large spoon and sprinkle them in the desired prepared location.

Other seeds germinate better after being submerged in hot water prior to planting. Place the seeds in a jar and fill it halfway with tap water that is hot to the touch, but not scalding. Allow the seeds to remain in the water as it cools overnight. The seeds can then be planted the next day.

Light or Dark Treatments. A few species of wildflowers have seeds that are either stimulated or inhibited by light. If the seeds are stimulated by light they should be planted shallowly, so sunlight penetrating through the surface of the soil can have its desired effect. If the seeds are inhibited by light, they should be planted at sufficient depth to prevent light from slowing germination.

PLANTING
TECHNIQUES

One of the most efficient ways to propagate wildflowers from seed is to use flats or nursery beds for rearing seedlings for the first year or until they become established. The advantage of flats is that you can transplant seedlings to holding beds and maintain an optimum density of plants more easily than if you plant the seed directly in the desired location. Also, some species have seed that is slow to germinate, and it may take several years for all the viable seeds that were planted to produce seedlings. The soil can be kept in the flats until the seeds have had sufficient time to germinate completely.

If you have only a few seeds, small pots can be used for raising seedlings. If the species is one that thrives in slightly acidic conditions, peat pots are a real convenience. When the seedlings are sturdy they can be transplanted to a nursery bed, where they can grow without competition from other plants, or to permanent locations. Be careful not to disturb the roots or to break off the shoots when removing the seedlings and soil from pots. If you are using peat pots, simply tear off the bottom of the pot and plant the container with its contents so that the surface level of the soil is the same as that inside the pot. (Unlike many gardeners, I tear off the bottom of the peat pot, because I have found the plant makes better contact with the soil that way.)

Soil Mixes and Potting. The soil in which a seed germinates and the seedling starts out is every bit as important as that in which the adult plant grows. A potting soil should have both good drainage and good water-holding capacity. While commercially formulated starting mixes are available from home and garden centers, you can make an inexpensive but effective mix by adding equal parts milled sphagnum, washed builder's sand, and potting soil. The resulting mix is weed-free and sterile. One convenient way to start seeds is to use 4½-by-6¼-inch plastic flats that are 2½ inches deep. Fill the flat to the top with the potting mix and then tamp down the surface, with the bottom of another flat, so that the soil surface is just below the rim. Set the seeds on the soil surface, and then cover them with the appropriate depth of additional soil. Moisten the soil with a fine sprinkle, and cover the top of the flat with plastic wrap to help conserve soil moisture. Leave the plastic on the flats until the seeds germinate and the tops of the seedlings are just pushing against the film.

Plugs and Sods. An effective way to grow live plants for transplanting to meadows is to produce wildflower *plugs* and sods. Plugs are individual live plants that have been grown in small pots or special trays. They can be efficiently transplanted into meadows or gardens because of their compact, dense mass of roots. They are most easily produced in special plug trays available through greenhouse supply companies and larger garden centers. These trays have cavities up to 2 inches in diameter and 2 inches deep with gently tapering sides so that the plugs can be easily removed.

To produce wildflower plugs, use the larger trays with 2-inch openings, and fill the cavities with potting mix as you would other pots or flats. Allow the seedlings to develop until the roots fully bind the soil in the cavities, a process that may take most of a growing season for some species. Water the plugs by periodically setting the entire tray in a shallow pan and allowing the water to be drawn up from the bottom. The wildflowers can be transplanted into the garden or meadow when a gentle tug at the base of the plant's stem pulls the entire plug, soil and all, out of the cavity.

Wildflower sods are like plugs, only larger. Sods can be made with a number of different wildflowers and grasses grown densely together in flats. You then transplant the entire contents of the flat into a meadow or garden. One way to make sods easier to handle is to line the flat with cheesecloth before adding the potting soil. The seeds are then planted in the soil, and as the seedlings mature their roots will penetrate the cloth liner. When it is time to transplant the sod, you can lift it out of the flat by pulling on the cheesecloth. Once in the ground, the roots of the sod plants will quickly grow through the cheese-cloth and after about a year the cloth will simply decompose.

A Special Note on Legumes. Members of the bean family often require the presence of special microorganisms, known as *rhizobia*, in the soil to ensure their survival. These microbes lead a symbiotic existence with these plants, inhabiting nodules formed on the root systems and producing nitrogen compounds that the plants eventually use. Not all soils have abundant populations of these necessary microbes. If you have difficulty in propagating leguminous wildflowers like lupines, you may need to purchase a commercially produced "inoculant" and add it to the soil when you plant the seeds. Different species require different strains of microbial inoculants, so the addition of "pea" or "soybean" inoculants would not necessarily be effective for wildflowers. Make sure you get the right strain of rhizobia for the species you plan to cultivate.

Rhizobia inoculants can be ordered directly from the Nitragin Company, Inc., 3101 W. Custer Avenue, Milwaukee, WI 53209, or Kalo, Inc., P.O. Box 12567, Columbus, OH 43212. You will need to indicate the scientific name of the species to be inoculated and the amount of seed you intend to treat. It may take two to four weeks for these companies to prepare special rhizobia if they are not in stock.

ROOTSTOCK
DIVISIONS

One of the quickest ways to propagate perennials is by rootstock division. Rootstocks are best dug up and divided while the plant is dormant. In general, perennials that flower in the spring can be most successfully divided in the fall, and those that flower in the fall are best divided in the early spring. For those species like western shooting star whose shoots wither and enter dormancy before the end of the growing season, the location of the plants should be marked with a stake so that the rootstocks can be found later in the fall for propagation.

Regardless of the type of rootstock (see illustration on pages 29 and 30) the principal technique is quite similar (see illustration on page 52). With a sharp knife (a pocket knife will do splendidly), cut the rootstock so that the divided pieces have at least one vegetative bud or "eye" attached. Since the size of the resulting plant will be determined to a large extent by the size of the divided piece, don't make the divisions too small (unless you want lots of tiny plants).

Runners and stolons are easily divided by cutting the horizontal stem between adjacent rooted plants, which can then be dug up and transplanted when dormant. The division of tubers is also easily accomplished. Cut tubers into pieces, each with a bud or two, and plant them with the buds pointing up (the way you would plant pieces of potato). New shoots and roots will be produced as the plant draws upon the energy reserves of the tuber flesh. Similarly rhizomes can be divided into pieces, each with buds and associated roots. Replant the segments at the appropriate depth and spacing.

Corms and bulbs of perennial wildflowers can be divided in a manner similar to other garden perennials. The small offsets that develop on the sides of mature corms and bulbs can be removed with a knife during the dormant season and planted at the appropriate depth. These cormlets and bulblets will usually take several years to develop into plants capable of flowering. If not cut off the parent rootstock, these offsets eventually mature into large, densely crowded plants that will benefit from being divided and given wider spacing.

Rootstock propagation.

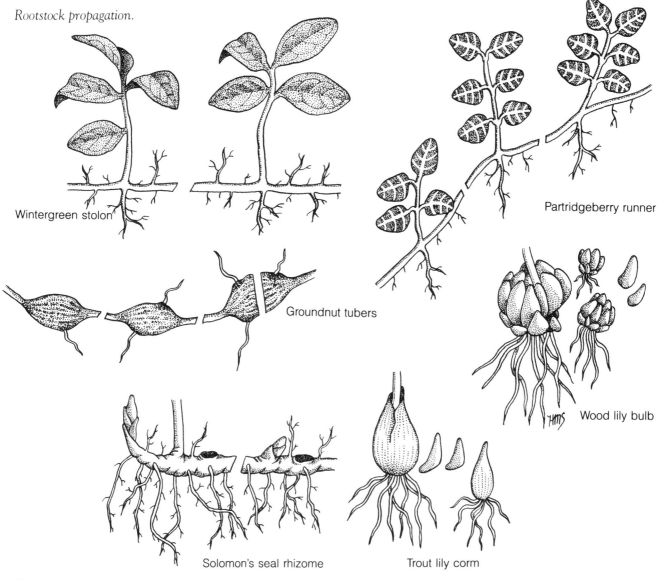

Wintergreen stolon

Partridgeberry runner

Groundnut tubers

Wood lily bulb

Solomon's seal rhizome

Trout lily corm

THE WILDFLOWER GARDENER'S GUIDE

The fleshy scales of bulbs such as lilies can be divided and planted like seeds in flats to produce large quantities of "seedlings." Break off the individual scales from dormant bulbs, and in a flat containing potting soil mixture, plant them just below the soil surface, with the tips of the scales pointing upward. Provide light shade and keep the soil moist, but not overly wet, until the resulting small plants are sturdy enough to transplant into a nursery bed or permanent location.

After replanting the rootstock divisions be especially careful not to overwater the soil. The soil should be prevented from thoroughly drying out, but wet soils may invite problems. Rootstocks have carbohydrate-rich stores of energy that the plant draws upon during its period of most rapid growth. If the soil is too wet, bacterial and fungal rots may attack the newly divided rootstock pieces and even kill the plants. For this reason, it is a good idea to plant rootstock divisions in a nursery or holding bed that has well-drained soil, and to transplant the stock when dormant the following year.

STEM CUTTINGS

Another successful way to propagate some perennials is to make cuttings of stems. These cuttings should be made when the shoots are growing vigorously and are most successful if the shoot lacks flower buds. The best time to make a cutting is when the plant has been well watered, by rain or artificial irrigation, especially in the early morning before the sun evaporates the water from the leaf surfaces.

Before making the cuttings prepare a flat with a mixture of coarse compost or sphagnum moss and builder's sand (don't use beach sand from the ocean, as the salt might kill the cuttings). Moisten the soil, poke holes 2 to 3 inches deep and 5 inches apart with your little finger, and take the flat to the garden. Select succulent stems that snap crisply when doubled over. Cut 6-inch pieces of rapidly growing shoots by making a diagonal slice through the stem with a razor blade. To encourage root formation, remove flower buds and leaves from the bottom 6 inches of the stem. Gently place the cutting into the hole and firmly press the soil around the base to assure good contact with the cutting. Then moisten the soil again.

Since the cuttings initially have no root systems, it is difficult for them to take up water. It is essential to keep the flats in the *shade* with the soil *moist* but not wet. Soils that are too wet will prevent oxygen from getting to the developing roots and will also encourage rotting diseases. Protect the cuttings from the effects of drying winds, and mist the plants if the humidity is low. To attain ideal humidity control, put the entire flat in a large, *clear* polyethylene bag (available from janitorial supply companies), and tie off the opening. Another idea is to use a clear plastic garment bag to create a mini-greenhouse for start-

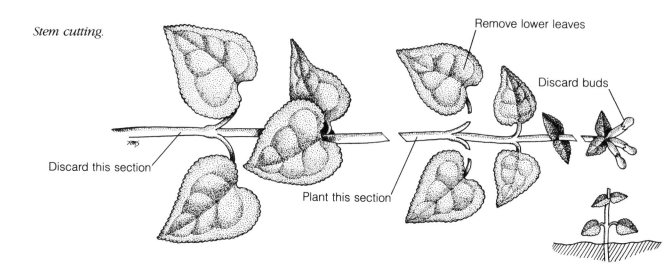

Stem cutting.

Remove lower leaves

Discard buds

Discard this section

Plant this section

ing cuttings. Allow the cuttings to remain in the flat until they go into dormancy at the end of the growing season, and then transplant them to holding beds or permanent locations.

Whether by collecting your own seeds or by dividing or cutting live plants, wildflower propagation can give you satisfactions beyond the considerable cost savings. Many perennials should be divided every several years, and they respond to this treatment by flowering more abundantly and adding even greater beauty to the garden. You can use the surplus divisions to enlarge your plantings, give them to other wildflower enthusiasts, or use them as material for container gardens. Perhaps one of the most important benefits of propagating plants yourself is the increased familiarity with wildflowers you gain in the process.

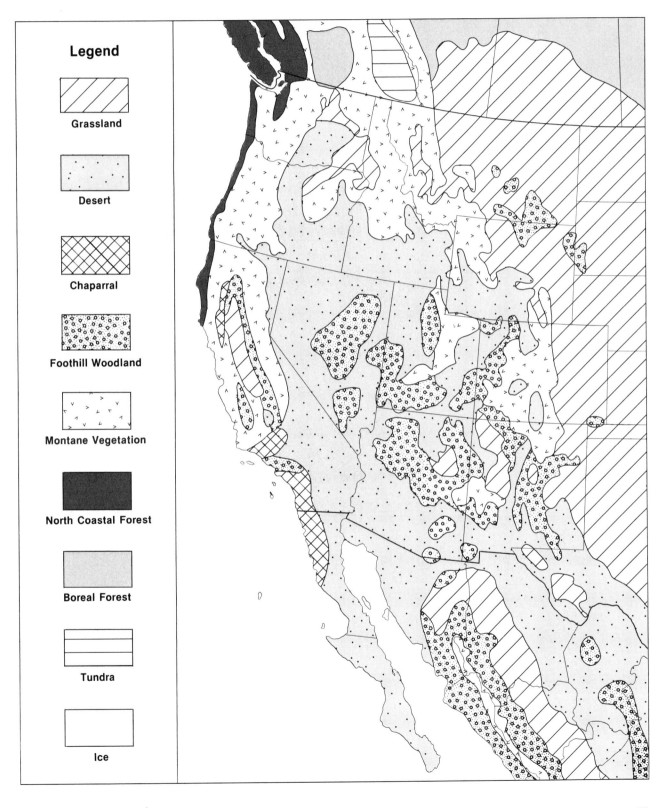

Legend

Grassland

Desert

Chaparral

Foothill Woodland

Montane Vegetation

North Coastal Forest

Boreal Forest

Tundra

Ice

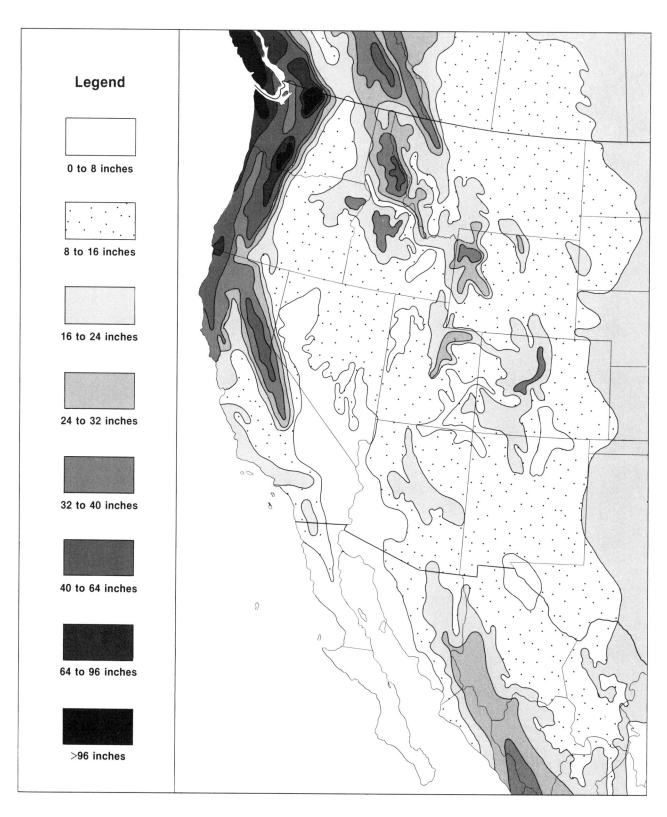

Legend

0 to 8 inches

8 to 16 inches

16 to 24 inches

24 to 32 inches

32 to 40 inches

40 to 64 inches

64 to 96 inches

>96 inches

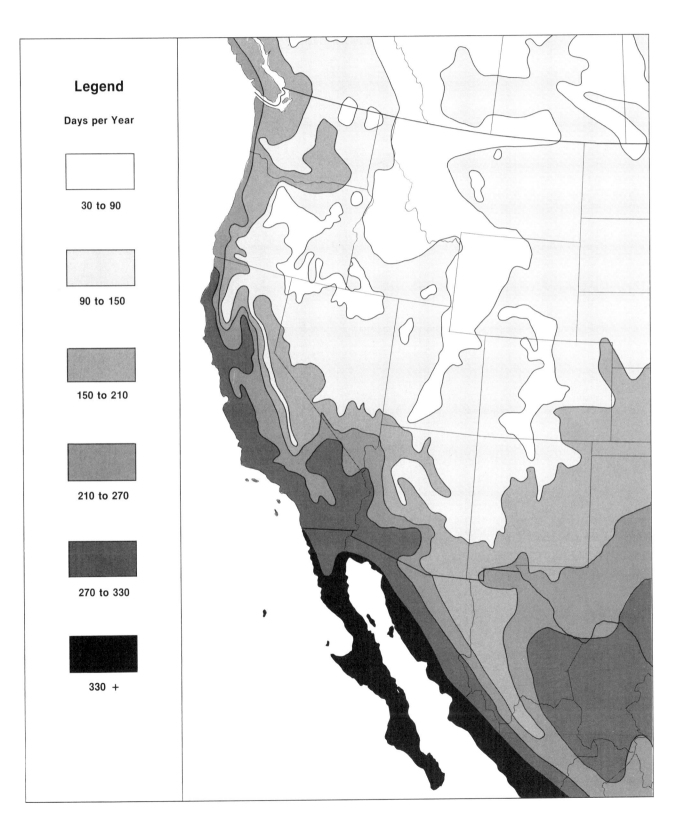

Legend

Days per Year

30 to 90

90 to 150

150 to 210

210 to 270

270 to 330

330 +

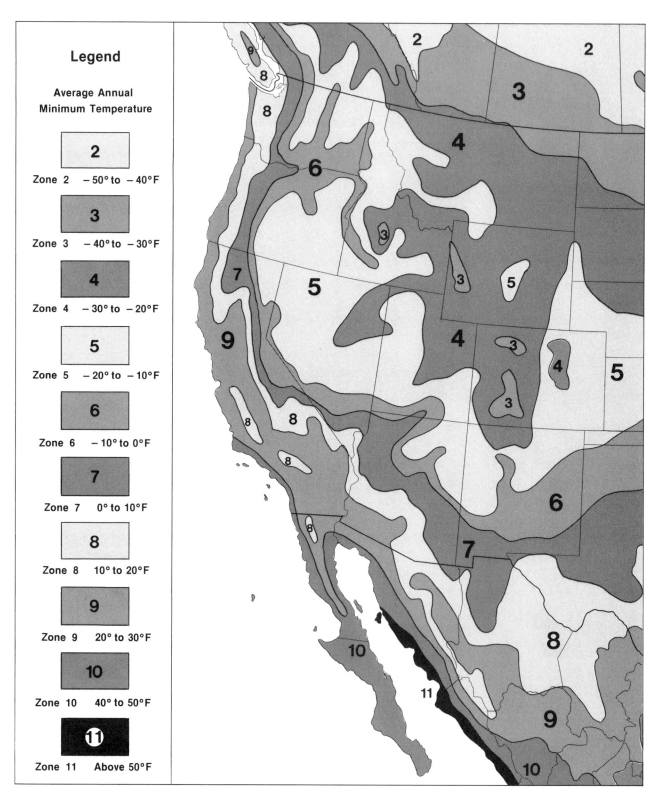

Legend

Average Annual Minimum Temperature

Zone 2   −50° to −40°F

Zone 3   −40° to −30°F

Zone 4   −30° to −20°F

Zone 5   −20° to −10°F

Zone 6   −10° to 0°F

Zone 7   0° to 10°F

Zone 8   10° to 20°F

Zone 9   20° to 30°F

Zone 10   40° to 50°F

Zone 11   Above 50°F

PART II

A Gallery of
Southwestern Wildflowers

Desert sand verbena, with its sticky leaves and clusters of bright pink flowers, creeps over desert gardens in the spring. (See page 80.)

The flat flower heads of the **desert marigold** fill the garden with gold for most of the growing season and, with proper watering, well into fall. (See page 82.)

The bright red flowers of **Eaton's firecracker** are pollinated by hummingbirds that hover below the narrow openings. (See page 84.)

Although **California bluebells** is native to southwestern deserts, it can be grown under a wide variety of garden conditions. (See page 86.)

The long stamens and pistils of **purple heliotrope** give the coiled cluster of flowers a lacy appearance. This adaptable desert species is sometimes grown as "bee food." (See page 88.)

The apricot-orange flowers of the **desert mallow** look like miniature hollyhocks. The fuzzy hairs on its stem and leaves can cause eye irritations. (See page 90.)

Southwestern verbena, with its compact clusters of lavender flowers, grows as a dense mat in garden settings as well as in its native deserts. (See page 92.)

Farewell-to-spring can be found with flowers ranging in color from red to pink to white. (See page 96.)

Like miniature pink cyclamen, **Western shooting stars** grace meadows and open woodlands in the early spring. (See page 98.)

Deep golden petals and masses of orange stamens distinguish the flowers of **California poppy** as they rise above the lacy blue-green foliage. (See page 100.)

The flowers of **Douglas's iris** range in color from tan to white to blue. A native of grasslands and open woodlands, it is also a popular addition to rock gardens or for borders. (See page 102.)

The small yellow flowers of **goldfields** blanket vast areas in its native grasslands. (See page 104.)

The ray florets of **tidy tips** are yellow and white, giving the flower heads of this grassland annual a striking appearance. It is seen here growing with meadow foam (*Limnanthes douglasii*). (See page 106.)

The **purple annual lupine** is a welcomed addition to the garden even though it has become a roadside plant in portions of the Southwest. (See page 108.)

Much of the showy color of **owl's clover** is due to the magenta bracts beneath the yellow and rose flowers. While it is usually a parasitic plant in grasslands, it can be grown easily in the garden. (See page 110.)

Checker bloom resembles a miniature pink hollyhock. It has long been a favorite for rock gardens because of its compact size. (See page 112.)

Blue-eyed grass is among the earliest wildflowers of southwestern grass-lands. Its foliage appears grasslike, although it is a member of the iris family. (See page 114.)

The red-orange flowers of **wind poppy** are borne atop 1–2-foot-high stems. This easy-to-grow annual is native to California grasslands and meadows. (See page 116.)

The crepe-paper-white petals of **prickly poppy** surround the mass of yellow stamens at the flower's center. The prickly, blue-green foliage provides a striking contrast to the soft flowers. (See page 120.)

Dense clusters of royal blue, lilylike flowers top the long, leafless stems of **blue dicks**. Its flower stems and grasslike foliage arise from a corm in the early spring. (See page 122.)

Golden yarrow's bright golden flowers accent its woolly gray-green leaves in the spring and early summer. This chaparral plant grows well on well-drained sites. (See page 124.)

Douglas's wallflower has flowers that range in color from yellow to orange to brick-red. A wonderfully adaptable plant for sunny locations. (See page 126.)

Up to 100 puffy pink flowers may mass atop the shoot of **showy penstemon**, a chaparral species of southern California. (See page 128.)

The white crowd of **Our Lord's candle** flowers open as its sole pollinator, the yucca moth, emerges in the late spring. A yucca moth can be seen gathering pollen in the flower above. Mounds of swordlike foliage (left), take up considerable room as plants reach flowering size. Spaces between the clumps can be planted with other wildflowers. (See page 130.)

71

Hummingbirds pollinate the bright red flowers of **California fuchsia.** This chaparral species is one of the few to flower in the late summer and early fall. (See page 132.)

Photograph taken at Rancho Santa Ana Botanic Garden, Claremont, CA.

The whorls of snapdragon-like flowers give **Chinese houses** a pagoda effect. This woodland plant grows best in partial shade. (See page 136.)

Clusters of deep pink flowers are borne atop the long, leafless stems of **coralbells.** The flower stems arise out of mounds of heart-shaped leaves. (See page 138.)

Linanthus, with its delicate pink flowers emerging from tufts of spiny leaves, is a beautiful addition to rock gardens in sunny sites. (See page 140.)

Lomatium emerges in the spring with clusters of small white flowers. By summer the flowers have produced attractive heads of winged seeds. (See page 142.)

Sky lupine often grows in masses in California grasslands, and is an excellent choice for planting in barren banks and open sites. (See page 144.)

The spectacular yellow flowers of **blazing star,** seen here growing with **farewell-to-spring,** open in the evening and usually close by noon the next day. (See page 146.)

Photograph taken at Rancho Santa Ana Botanic Garden, Claremont, CA.

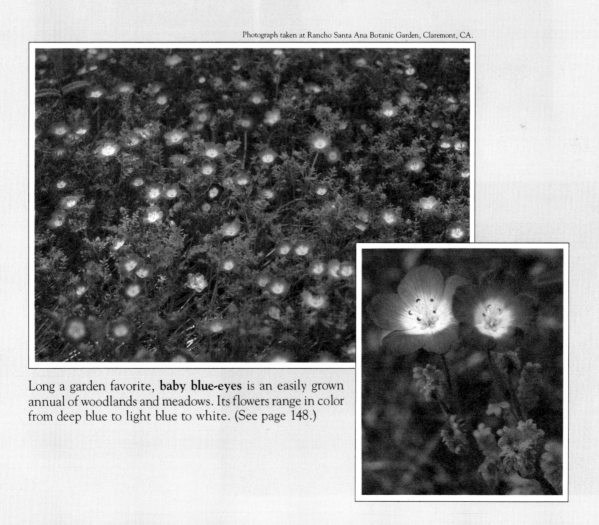

Long a garden favorite, **baby blue-eyes** is an easily grown annual of woodlands and meadows. Its flowers range in color from deep blue to light blue to white. (See page 148.)

Giant evening primrose is an excellent choice for filling large spaces in sites where the soil is moist. This biennial's flowers open in the evening and wither by noon the next day. (See page 150.)

The bright red flowers of **Indian pink** have five broad petals, each dissected into four round-tipped lobes. The soft stems are covered with minute, sticky hairs. (See page 152.)

PART III

Species of Wildflowers

The following pages give detailed information about 36 species of wildflowers. The plants are grouped by their natural habitat and appear in alphabetical order by botanical names. Wildflowers within the groups can grow together as companions, but many of the species can grow in more than one habitat. Each habitat group is introduced by general comments, a wildflower garden plan, and suggestions of additional species not in this edition of *The Wildflower Gardener's Guide* that make appropriate companions. Further information on these companions can be found in *A Garden of Wildflowers* or other books listed in Appendix D.

Each of the 36 wildflowers included in this book is listed by its most frequently used common name as well as by its Latin scientific name. Other common English, Spanish, and Native American names are also given. The individual wildflower description starts with general information about the species and its ecology. A discussion of culture and growth requirements follows, with specific directions for the plant's propagation. A few companions that grow under similar conditions are listed.

Each species is illustrated. A scale shows the approximate size of the plant, and a quick reference box shows plant family, flower color, flowering and fruiting time, growth cycle (annual, biennial, or perennial), habitats where the species naturally occurs, and hardiness zones where the species can be grown. The map shows the wildflower's native distribution, but most species can be grown over a much wider area.

DESERT SPECIES

The species presented in this section are adapted to survival in the sunny, drought-prone conditions of southwestern deserts. Although these species are native to the desert they are also adaptable to many grassland, chaparral, and foothill garden situations, especially where you wish to reduce water consumption by xeriscaping. Designing a native garden in the desert is both challenging and rewarding. Rainfall collected by the roofs of dwellings can be an excellent source of supplemental irrigation for the garden, and planning the position of gardens relative to buildings is an essential step in reducing water consumption. The flowering season of some wildflowers can be extended by supplemental watering, but others are likely to rot with too much moisture.

Although none are presented in this book, succulents are a natural component of desert gardens, especially in the hot Mojave, Colorado, and Sonoran deserts, which lack intensely cold winters. Cacti provide points of visual interest through their variety of shapes, textures, and even their spectacular, though short-lived, flowers. They are typically slow growing, so be patient and plant them several feet apart with interplantings of wildflowers. DO NOT COLLECT CACTI FROM THE WILD; purchase nursery-propagated plants from reputable dealers.

A few suggestions: The **golden barrel cactus** (*Echinocactus grusonii*) is a rotund native of Mexico that is capable of slowly growing to 4 feet high and 3 feet in diameter. Its attractive yellow flowers appear briefly in the spring, but its large, translucent, golden spines contrast with its deep green skin throughout the year. The **beavertail cactus** (*Opuntia basilaris*) has trailing, flattened, nearly spineless, padlike stems that may grow to several feet in height. There are several varieties of this species, with flower colors ranging from cerise to yellow. The **teddy bear cholla** or **hedgehog cactus** (*Opuntia bigelovii*) is a related species, but has a very different form. Its 2–6-foot-high, branched, tubular stem is covered with unforgiving white spines that glow brilliantly in the early morning and late afternoon sun.

If your garden is large enough, consider planting native shrubs or trees to complement the wildflowers. **Mormon tea** (*Ephedra virens*), a shrub of the Great

Southwestern hot desert garden

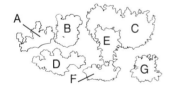

A. Southwestern verbena
B. Purple heliotrope
C. Desert mallow
D. Desert sand verbena
E. Eaton's firecracker
F. Desert marigold
G. California bluebell

Basin, can withstand cold winters as well as summer heat. Its thin, tubular, evergreen stems have minute leaves and bear clusters of small green-yellow flowers. **Sagebrush** (*Artemesia tridentata*) is another Great Basin shrub that not only fills the air with its pungent fragrance, but also provides a superb year-round gray-green backdrop for brightly colored desert wildflowers.

Desert willow (*Chilopsis linearis*) is a large shrub or small tree that grows to 20 feet. In the spring this relative of the catalpa tree bears puffy pink flowers and narrow, willowlike leaves. By late summer only cigar-shaped fruits remain suspended from the light tan branches. Another similar-sized species is the **blue palo verde** (*Cercidium floridum*) whose bright yellow flowers and smooth green leaves are shed early, but whose bark and spiny branches remain green throughout the year. Finally, the wandlike stems of **ocotillo** (*Fouquieria splendens*), another native shrub, typically grow 8–15 feet high, but may occasionally reach 25 feet. After the winter rainy season the stems become densely covered with lush, spatula-shaped leaves, and clusters of bright scarlet flowers appear at the tips of the branches. The flowers and leaves wither at the onset of the summer dry season, leaving the stark stems looking rather dead but still attractive, especially when silhouetted at dawn and dusk.

DESERT SAND VERBENA

Abronia villosa

(Lilac sand verbena, wild lantana, *alfombrilla*)

During those springs when the desert blooms, this annual carpets the hottest and driest parts of the Mojave, Colorado, and Sonoran deserts with mounds of fragrant, lavender-pink flowers. It is not a verbena at all, but a member of the four o'clock family. Desert sand verbena appears as a mat following winter rains, growing to 20 inches across and inspiring the Spanish common name *alfombrilla* ("little carpet"). Short sticky hairs cover both the inch-long, oval, fleshy leaves and the many-branched stems and often trap grains of sand. By early spring desert sand verbena sends up 1–3-inch-long stems bearing rounded clusters of 5 to 15 flowers. The Latin name *Abronia* is from the Greek *Abros* meaning "delicate," describing the fragile, elongated involucre bracts that surround the flower clusters. The ½-inch-long flowers lack petals, but the 5-lobed, rose-to-lilac-hued calyx is every bit as attractive and may persist for up to 2 months. The dry capsule fruits of desert sand verbena look like dark brown toy tops with wings. When mature, the fruits and their cargoes of small seeds are blown off the plant and spin across the desert to new locations. They can float for several days, should they be caught in a flash flood, and can germinate even after being soaked in salty water or lying dormant in the soil for many years. Even though desert sand verbena is an annual, it may form an extensive root system, spreading as much as 3 feet from the center of the mat of foliage and a foot or more deep into the soil.

CULTURE

Desert sand verbena requires well-drained soils and sunny locations. While it is quite heat- and drought-tolerant, it will have a prolonged growth and flowering season if additional water is provided. This is an excellent plant for coastal and desert gardens as well as for open borders, banks and walls, rock gardens, and hanging baskets. It can be used as an effective annual ground cover in hardiness zones 8–10 since it self-seeds.

PROPAGATION

Plant the seeds 1/8–1/4 inch deep in the late summer, fall, or early spring, either in pots or in desired locations. Germination may be enhanced if you remove the seeds from the papery fruit just before planting them. Keep seeds moist until germination starts, usually in about 3 weeks. If late summer rains have been ample, flowering may start in late fall and continue through to the following summer. If seedlings have been started in pots, do not wait too long before transplanting them to outdoor locations since they will quickly develop extensive root systems.

COMPANIONS

California bluebells, golden yarrow, Douglas's wallflower, desert mallow, desert marigold, southwestern verbena.

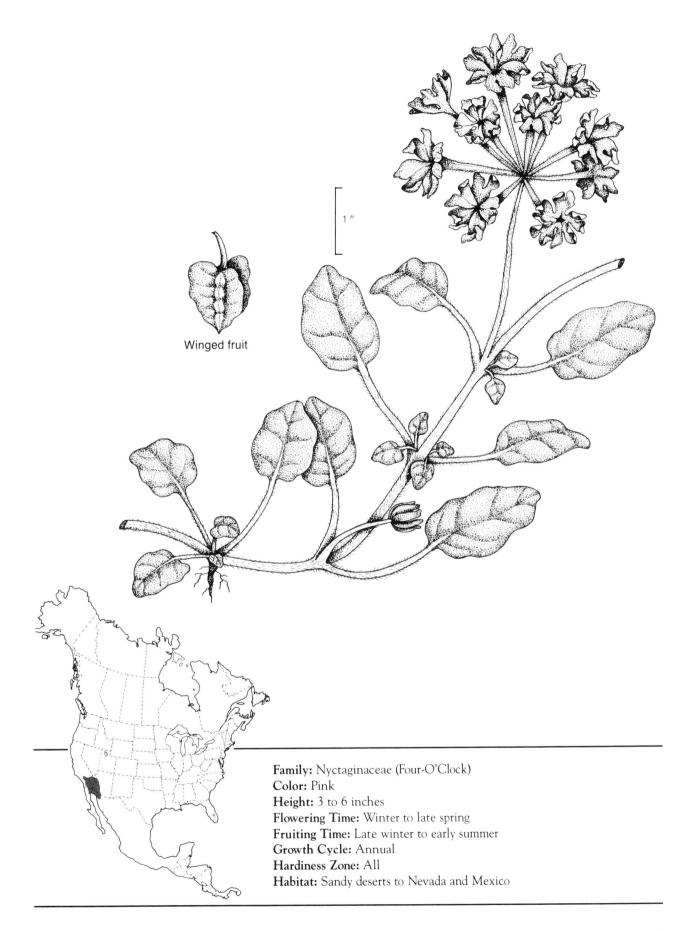

Winged fruit

Family: Nyctaginaceae (Four-O'Clock)
Color: Pink
Height: 3 to 6 inches
Flowering Time: Winter to late spring
Fruiting Time: Late winter to early summer
Growth Cycle: Annual
Hardiness Zone: All
Habitat: Sandy deserts to Nevada and Mexico

DESERT SAND VERBENA (*Abronia villosa*)

DESERT MARIGOLD

Baileya multiradiata

(Desert baileya, wild marigold)

This woolly plant of the southwestern deserts can fill the garden with mounds of brilliant yellow for almost the entire growing season. Both the stems and the broadly lobed, 1½–3-inch-long, gray-green leaves are densely covered with silky hairs. Most of the leaves are toward the base of the stems, the top half of the scape lacking foliage entirely. Single 1–2-inch flower heads top the 12–16-inch stems. The numerous (25–50), ½-inch-long ray flowers have 3 to 5 teeth on their blunt tips and overlap each other in several layers. As the equally brilliant yellow disc flowers produce small, grooved, columnar, seedlike fruits, the ray flowers lose their brilliance, droop, and turn a papery white. Desert marigold is poisonous to sheep and goats.

CULTURE   Desert marigold flowers in the spring in its native low deserts from the eastern Mojave to Utah. It will bloom into the fall, however, if given sufficient but not too much moisture. Since this species is subject to crown rot if the soil is too wet, allow the soil surface to dry out before watering. It is essential to plant the seeds in open, sunny locations on dry, well-drained soils. Although clayey loams are acceptable in desert areas, gritty sands are preferable in the more humid areas of the Southwest. This is an excellent plant for rock gardens and requires little attention.

PROPAGATION   Although desert marigold grows as a biennial or perennial in its native habitat, it should be grown as an annual from seed elsewhere. Plant the seeds ¼ inch deep in the garden in the fall or spring. The easiest method is to scatter the seeds on the soil surface and gently rake them in. Water gently until germination starts and then reduce the watering. Alternatively, you can start the seeds indoors in flats or peat pots filled with sandy loam and transplant them outdoors when all danger of frost has passed. The seeds do not require cold treatment in order to germinate.

COMPANIONS   Southwestern verbena, desert sand verbena, desert mallow, purple heliotrope, California bluebells.

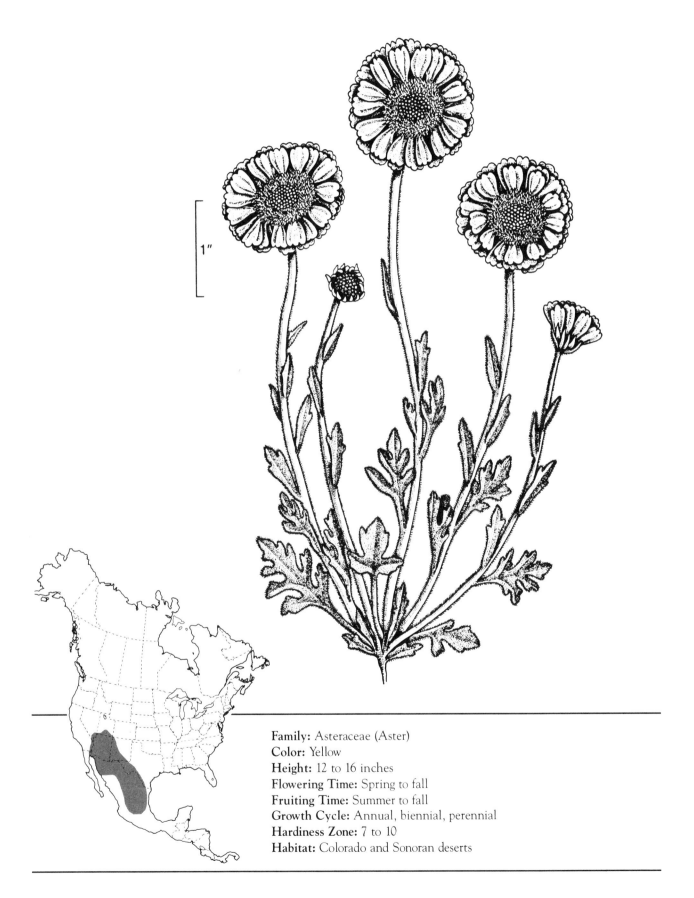

Family: Asteraceae (Aster)
Color: Yellow
Height: 12 to 16 inches
Flowering Time: Spring to fall
Fruiting Time: Summer to fall
Growth Cycle: Annual, biennial, perennial
Hardiness Zone: 7 to 10
Habitat: Colorado and Sonoran deserts

DESERT MARIGOLD (*Baileya multiradiata*)

EATON'S FIRECRACKER

Penstemon eatonii

(Firecracker penstemon, scarlet bugler)

These blazing wands of dangling scarlet firecrackers, growing on dry, rocky slopes in the Mojave Desert and Great Basin, are named after D.C. Eaton, a 19th-century professor of botany at Yale University. The tough, leathery, deep green leaves have wavy edges and are arranged in pairs along the coarse, purplish stems. The 3-inch-long lower leaves have distinct stalks, while the inch-long upper leaves clasp directly to the stem. Each of the several 1–2½-feet-high stems bears 5–10 carmine red flowers, which bloom in succession from the bottom toward the top during the spring and early summer. As with other penstemons, Eaton's firecracker has 5-lobed, tubular corollas surrounding 4 fertile stamens and a sterile one that projects out with a tuft of yellow hairs. But unlike most other penstemons, this species' thin, odorless flowers lack "landing platforms" and droop downward, making it difficult for insects to enter. Hummingbirds, however, hovering below the inch-long flowers, have little trouble in extracting the nectar. In the process, pollen sticks to the hummingbird's beak and is efficiently transferred to the next flower that is visited. The fruit of Eaton's firecracker is a capsule containing 1/16-inch-long seeds resembling small, brown-black raisins.

CULTURE

Grow Eaton's firecracker in full sun on well-drained soils. While this is a drought-tolerant perennial, its flowering season is prolonged by additional watering during the late spring and early summer. Eaton's firecracker is an excellent choice for dry, gravelly banks and for background plantings.

PROPAGATION

Eaton's firecracker is most successfully propagated by seed, although root divisions are also possible. Seeds germinate best after receiving cold treatment. If you live in a region colder than hardiness zone 9, plant the seeds ¼ inch deep in the fall and they will stratify naturally over the winter. In hardiness zones 9 and 10, stratify the seeds at 40°F for 1 to 2 months in the fall and then plant them either in the desired location or in pots for raising plants to transplant in the early spring. Root divisions in the late fall are another means of propagating this species. Divide the rootstock, being sure that each division has at least one shoot bud, and plant the segments with the bud just at the soil surface.

COMPANIONS

Prickly poppy, desert mallow, purple heliotrope, blue dicks, golden yarrow, California bluebells.

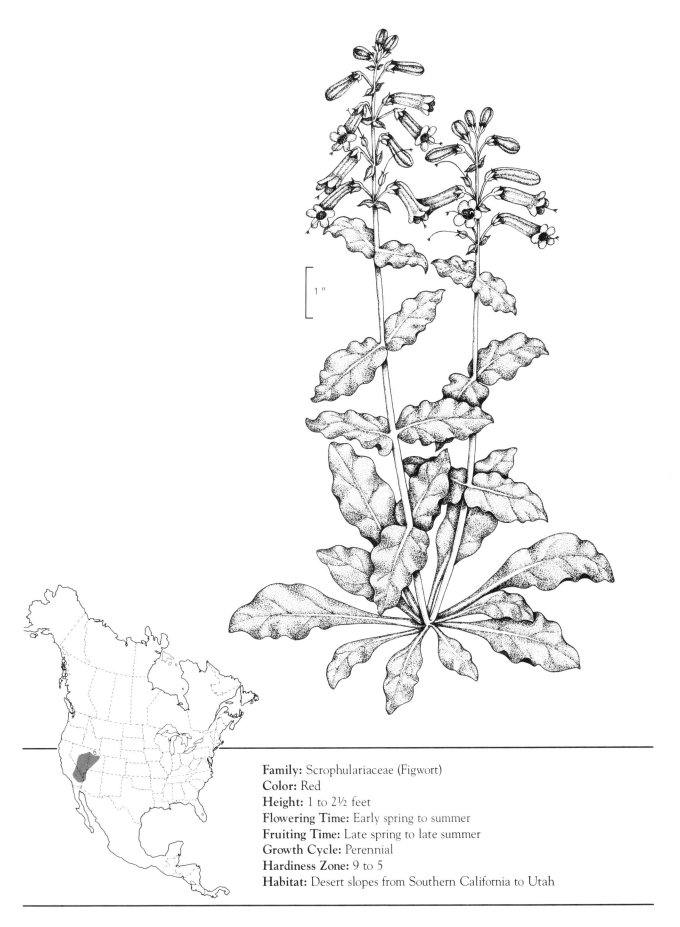

Family: Scrophulariaceae (Figwort)
Color: Red
Height: 1 to 2½ feet
Flowering Time: Early spring to summer
Fruiting Time: Late spring to late summer
Growth Cycle: Perennial
Hardiness Zone: 9 to 5
Habitat: Desert slopes from Southern California to Utah

EATON'S FIRECRACKER *(Penstemon eatonii)*

CALIFORNIA BLUEBELLS
Phacelia campanularia

(Desert bells, desert bluebells, blue bells)

Showy carpets of California bluebells cover sunny hillsides in the Mojave and Colorado deserts. This species is a member of the waterleaf family, even though the shape of its flowers resembles those of the bluebell family. Plants vary in height, ranging from around 6 inches for those grown in full sunlight to nearly 2 feet for those grown in partial shade. The inch-long leaves are round to oval with coarse teeth, and both they and the reddish stems are covered with fine glandular hairs, which give some people a mild rash if touched. The ½–1-inch-long, deep blue, vase-shaped flowers are born in loose clusters at the ends of generally creeping stems. Just as the tubular corolla starts to open, 5 stamens with golden anthers spring forth. Then, as the flowers mature, an elongated, clefted, white style grows through the cluster of stamens. There is considerable variation in the shade of the blue, the shape of the flowers, and the form of the plant, several subspecies being recognized by botanists. The fruit is a small, pointed, egg-shaped capsule containing many 1/16-inch-long seeds.

CULTURE California bluebells grow best on sandy, well-drained, even nutrient-poor soils in full sun, when the days are hot and the nights are cool. Although a plant of deserts and semi-arid grasslands, this highly adaptable annual has long been a favorite in English gardens. The usual March-to-April flowering season may be prolonged into June if the weather is on the cool side, but is curtailed if it is too hot. This easy-to-grow wildflower is not as delicate as it looks.

PROPAGATION Propagate California bluebells from seed planted in the fall in hardiness zones 9 and 10 and in the early spring in colder regions. The seeds require no special treatment; just rake them lightly into the surface of the soil to place them the desired 1/8 inch deep. Seeds germinate best when the soil temperature is below 60°F, and then grow quickly and produce long-lasting flowers. For optimum flowering, thin the plants to 6–8 inches apart. Serial plantings at monthly intervals may further prolong the flowering season in the cooler portions of the Southwest.

COMPANIONS California poppy, owl's clover, tidy tips, golden yarrow, purple annual lupine, showy penstemon, Eaton's firecracker, desert marigold.

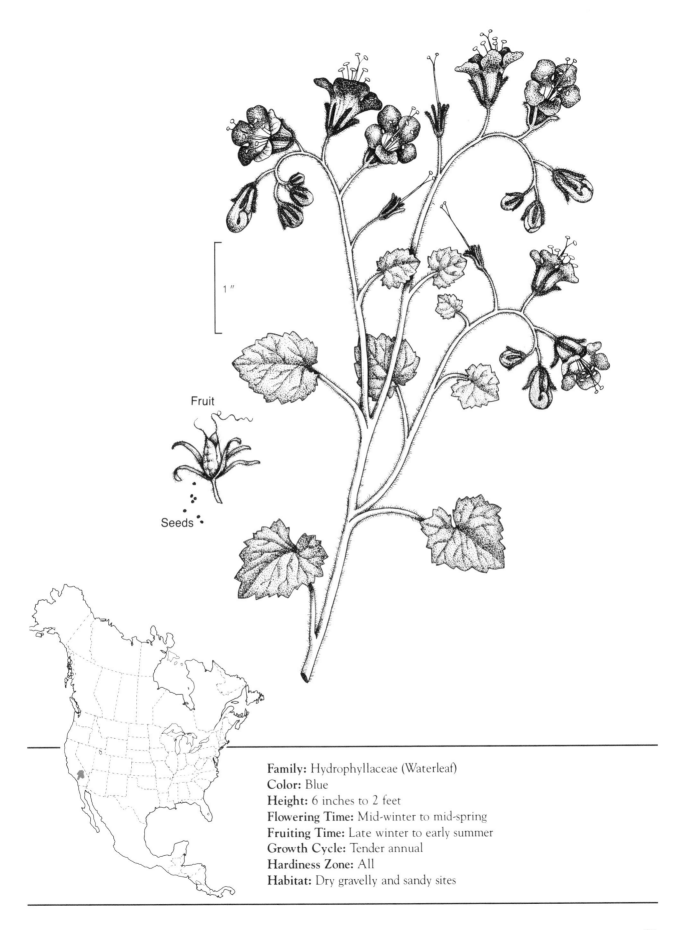

1 ″

Fruit

Seeds

Family: Hydrophyllaceae (Waterleaf)
Color: Blue
Height: 6 inches to 2 feet
Flowering Time: Mid-winter to mid-spring
Fruiting Time: Late winter to early summer
Growth Cycle: Tender annual
Hardiness Zone: All
Habitat: Dry gravelly and sandy sites

CALIFORNIA BLUEBELLS *(Phacelia campanularia)*

PURPLE HELIOTROPE

Phacelia tanacetifolia

(Bee food, lacy phacelia, tansy phacelia, *vervenia*)

This tall, erect annual has long been a favorite both as an ornamental in western gardens and as an agricultural crop in Europe and Australia, where it is planted to feed bees, although it has become a weed in parts of Eastern Europe. The 1–3-foot-high stems and the divided, feathery, clasping, tansylike leaves are covered with short, stiff hairs. The ½-inch-wide lavender-blue flowers, in fiddlehead clusters near the tops of the stems, emit a cloverlike fragrance that attracts numerous honeybees, hence the common name "bee food." Long-filamented stamens and deeply clefted styles extend well beyond the throats of the 5-lobed, bell-shaped flowers. The fruits are round ⅛-inch capsules containing 2 rounded, gray-brown, 1/16-inch seeds. Early Spanish settlers in the Southwest treated fever by making a bitter tea from the leaves of purple heliotrope.

CULTURE

Cultivate purple heliotrope in full sun on well-drained soils. The soil should be moist early in the spring and as the plants are becoming established, and then it can be allowed to dry out.

PROPAGATION

This annual is propagated only from seeds. While no stratification treatment is needed, germination of the seeds is strongly inhibited by the light as long as the seed coat is intact. For proper germination, scarify the seeds by rubbing them between two sheets of medium-grit sandpaper, or by carefully nicking the seeds with a sharp knife. Then soak the seeds overnight in water. Optimum germination temperature is a relatively cool 60°F and seeds can sprout in as few as 4 to 5 days. In purple heliotrope's natural range, seeds should be planted ⅛ inch deep in the late fall. Elsewhere plant the seeds in the early spring as the soil temperature nears 60°F.

COMPANIONS

Blazing star, linanthus, Douglas's wallflower, Eaton's firecracker, desert mallow, desert marigold.

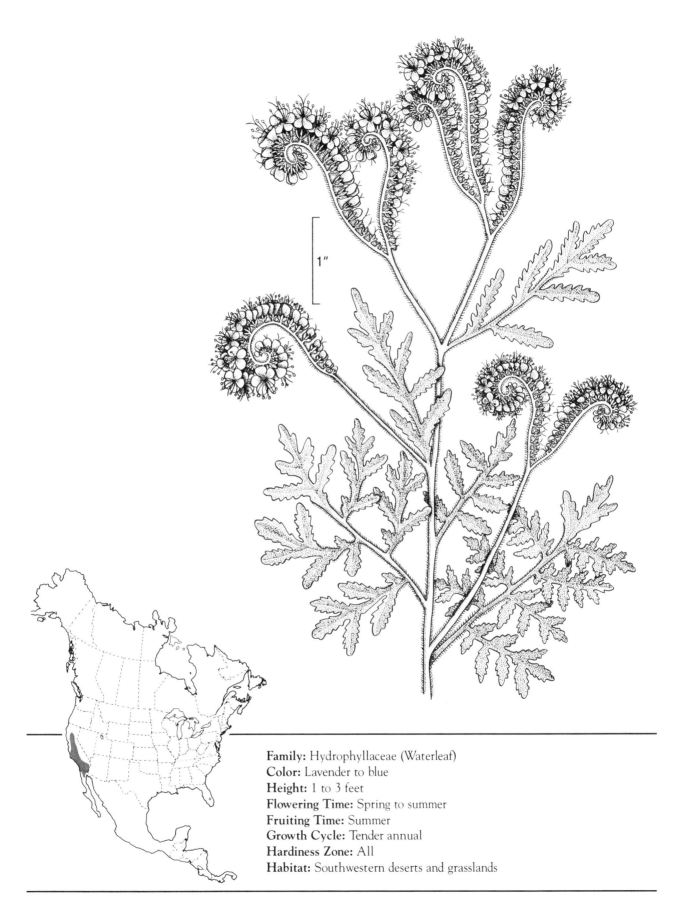

Family: Hydrophyllaceae (Waterleaf)
Color: Lavender to blue
Height: 1 to 3 feet
Flowering Time: Spring to summer
Fruiting Time: Summer
Growth Cycle: Tender annual
Hardiness Zone: All
Habitat: Southwestern deserts and grasslands

PURPLE HELIOTROPE *(Phacelia tanacetifolia)*

DESERT MALLOW

Sphaeralcea ambigua

(Desert hollyhock, *planta muy mala*)

With flowers resembling miniature vermilion hollyhocks, the desert mallow adds a splash of springtime orange to the Mojave Desert and cold deserts of the Southwest. This somewhat shrubby perennial grows 1½–3 feet high, with both stems and leaves densely covered with gray hairs. Although not a poppy at all, it is locally known as "sore-eye poppy," and in Spanish as "very bad plant," because the hairs are irritating to the eyes. The maplelike 1–2½ inch leaves have 3 rounded lobes and rounded, scalloped edges. Numerous ½–1½-inch-wide red-orange flowers are scattered about near the tips of the branched stems. Each of the flowers has 5 petals and many stamens that clasp the elongated style. The fruits are in a hemispherical arrangement with 12 to 16 segments attached at their bases in the center of the flower, each ¼-inch segment having a notch on the inside containing two seeds. The main root system is shallow and somewhat woody.

CULTURE

This hardy perennial can endure both freezing winter temperatures and the desert heat of summer. It should be grown in the full sun on well-drained, sandy soils. Although it is a plant of arid environments, it benefits from late fall and winter moisture.

PROPAGATION

Desert mallow should be propagated by seed. While the seeds require no stratification, they respond to late fall and winter rains. Plant the seeds ¼ inch deep in the fall in the desired locations. Usually they will germinate over winter and grow rapidly in the spring. Some flowers may be produced the first year and abundant flowering will occur the second. Desert mallow is relatively short-lived and may need to be replanted every several years, but it usually self-seeds.

COMPANIONS

Douglas's wallflower, desert sand verbena, desert marigold, golden yarrow, purple heliotrope, Eaton's firecracker.

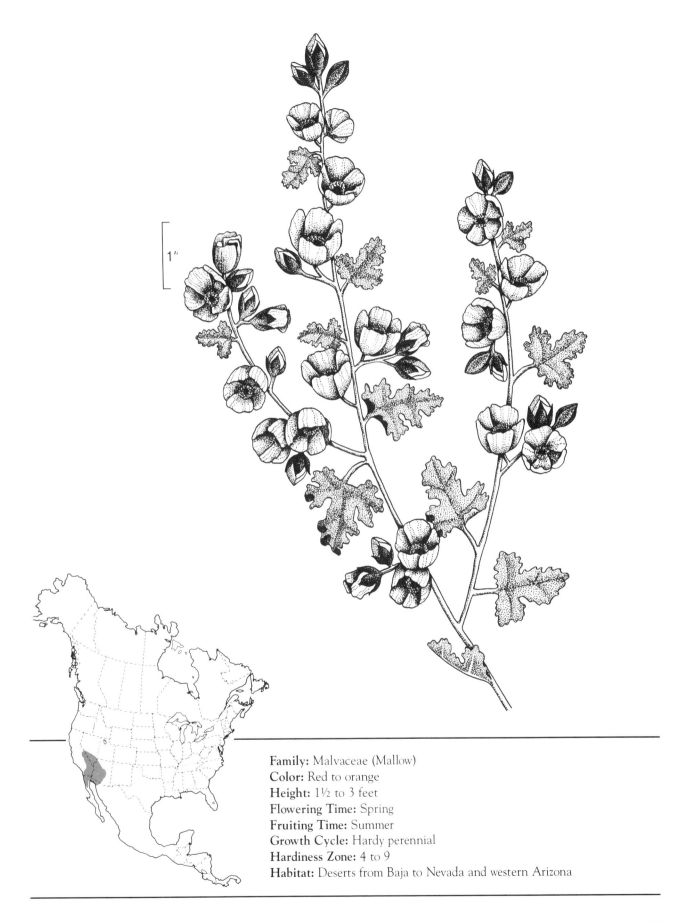

Family: Malvaceae (Mallow)
Color: Red to orange
Height: 1½ to 3 feet
Flowering Time: Spring
Fruiting Time: Summer
Growth Cycle: Hardy perennial
Hardiness Zone: 4 to 9
Habitat: Deserts from Baja to Nevada and western Arizona

DESERT MALLOW *(Sphaeralcea ambigua)*

91

SOUTHWESTERN VERBENA *Verbena gooddingii*

(Gooding's verbena, southwestern vervain)

This low verbena, a short-lived perennial, grows on sandy soils and in the mountains from the Mojave Desert in California to Texas. Both the stems and the deeply divided, 3-lobed leaves are quite hairy. It tends to spread, forming a sprawling green mat punctuated by broad, rounded clusters of about a dozen lavender flowers atop the several 6–8-inch scapes. Individual tubular flowers are ¾–1 inch wide with 5 petals, the one in the lower middle sometimes larger than the others and more conspicuously notched. Each of the flowers produces 4 narrow 1/8-inch-long nutlets.

CULTURE
The flowering season of southwestern verbena is dependent upon moisture and temperature. In California it blooms from April to June, while in other regions it may flower as early as February or as late as October. Southwestern verbena is quite drought tolerant and requires little water to maintain itself. Moderate watering, however, will prolong the flowering season in regions prone to summer aridity. It can tolerate moist soils well if the drainage is sufficient, but should be planted in the full sun. Irrigation, if any, should be done in the morning to allow the leaves to dry out. Southwestern verbena is an ideal ground cover for hot and dry locations, especially on banks.

PROPAGATION
Propagate southwestern verbena from seed. The seeds require no chilling treatment, but may germinate better if exposed to light. In hardiness zones 9 and 10, simply plant them 1/8–1/4 inch deep in the desired location in the early spring, and thin plants to 8–12 inches apart before they bloom in the summer. In colder regions this half-hardy perennial can be grown as an annual, started indoors in the late winter and transplanted to permanent locations when all danger of frost has passed. If grown as a perennial, apply a substantial layer of mulch in the fall, and remove it the following spring. In its native range, southwestern verbena will reseed itself once established.

COMPANIONS
Desert sand verbena, Eaton's firecracker, purple heliotrope.

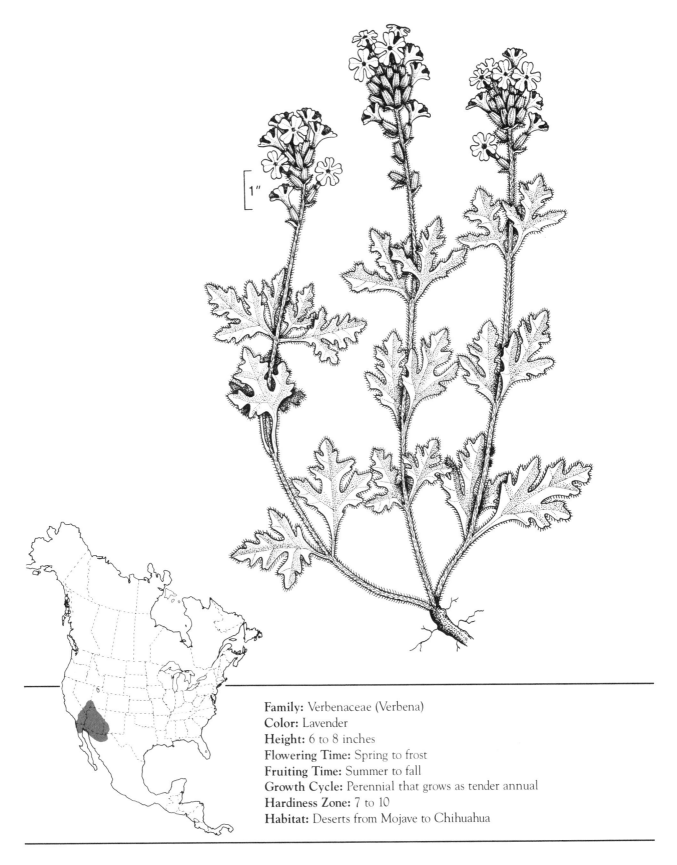

Family: Verbenaceae (Verbena)
Color: Lavender
Height: 6 to 8 inches
Flowering Time: Spring to frost
Fruiting Time: Summer to fall
Growth Cycle: Perennial that grows as tender annual
Hardiness Zone: 7 to 10
Habitat: Deserts from Mojave to Chihuahua

SOUTHWESTERN VERBENA *(Verbena gooddingii)*

GRASSLAND SPECIES

This section includes species that are native to both the coastal prairies bordering the Pacific Ocean and the interior grasslands bordering the foothills and deserts. Most of these wildflowers bloom in the spring and require full sun, although **western shooting star** and **Douglas's iris** grow well in the shade. All of the species in this section are adaptable to conventional garden situations, and many have been in the horticultural trade so long that their seeds are available from garden shops.

Be sure to include native grasses when designing grassland meadows (see page 20). *Stipa* and *Poa* species are well suited to interior grasslands, while *Festuca* and *Calamagrostis* are ideal for coastal prairies. Even though southwestern grasslands are dormant and brown from early summer to early winter, these native grasses provide visual interest through their varied forms and subtle color shadings.

The choices of commercially available grassland species that can complement these wildflowers are staggering. Many species presented in other sections of this book also can be grown in a mixed grassland garden and can help enrich the colors of the meadow palette: the deep blues of **California bluebells**, the light lavender of **purple heliotrope**, the medium blues of **blue dicks** swaying like brushes in the wind, the brilliant yellow of **blazing stars**, and the sky blue and cloud white of **sky lupine**.

Other annuals that make excellent additions to the southwestern wildflower meadow include **Creamcups** (*Platystemon californicus*), a 6-inch-high member of the poppy family whose 5 creamy petals are splashed with yellow at the base, and **birds-eye gilia** (*Gilia tricolor*), whose funnel-shaped flowers have yellow throats, violet lobes, and dark purple tips. Insects find these color combinations irresistible, and so will you. Cream cups and birds-eye gilia are especially effective when mixed with deeply hued species such as **California bluebells** and **wind poppy** or brightly colored species such as **California poppy, tidy tips**, and **goldfields.** Both self-seed once established and are very easy to grow.

California grassland meadow

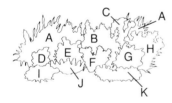

A. Purple needlegrass
B. Purple annual lupine
C. Wind poppy
D. California poppy
E. Blue dicks
F. Blue-eyed grass
G. Pine bluegrass
H. Blazing star
I. Tidy tips
J. Owl's clover
K. Goldfields

California golden violet or **Johnny jump-ups** (*Viola pedunculata*), a perennial that grows well in moister grasslands below 2,500 feet, has large (up to 1½ inches), yellow, pansy-like flowers with dark brown throats that guide its insect pollinators. It makes a stunning complement to **western shooting star**, both in the wild and in the garden. **Golden stars** (*Bloomeria crocea*) is a perennial that showers Southern California grasslands with clusters of bright yellow flowers in the late spring. It makes an attractive companion to **blue dicks** since it is also 1–2-feet high and arises from a crocus-like corm.

Blue flax (*Linum lewisii*), a widely distributed perennial of western North America, is closely related to the European species from which linen is made. It bears small clusters of 1½-inch sky blue flowers that arch to one side of the 1–3-foot-high stems. The leaves of blue flax are small and dark green, causing the stem to blend in with the spring grasses. **Butterfly weed** (*Asclepias tuberosa*) is a frequent component of desert grasslands in the Southwest and its range extends even into the Great Plains and the Midwest. As its common name suggests, its clusters of light orange flowers attract butterflies. The large, tuberous root system of this species makes it an excellent choice for dry sites. Since there is considerable geographic variation in this wildflower, purchase seeds or live plants from southwestern suppliers who sell regional native plants.

FAREWELL-TO-SPRING

Clarkia amoena
(Godetia amoena)

(Summer's darling, herald-of-summer, godetia, *adios primavera*)

Many of this plant's common names — farewell-to-spring, *adios primavera*, herald-of-summer, and summer's darling — refer to its flowering at the end of the spring and beginning of the summer. Native to coastal California and Oregon, this annual is named in honor of Captain William Clark, and not long after the Lewis and Clark expedition *Clarkia* was introduced by the Scottish botanist David Douglas into Europe as a garden flower. Much horticultural manipulation of this species has followed, and many varieties are now available through seed catalogs. Farewell-to-spring stands 1½–2½ feet tall and has linear, 1–3-inch-long leaves scattered along its stem. In the notches of several of the uppermost leaves are pink, cup-shaped, 2–4-inch flowers with 4 fan-shaped petals, blotched with dark red at their bases. White and lavender forms of this species also occur. Below the flowers are 4 reddish sepals, which often remain attached by their tips even after the flower bud has opened. In the center of the flower a 4-part white stigma tops the pistil, and 8 stamens rest against the petals. The flowers usually open during the day and close at night. The tapering, 1–2-inch-long capsular fruit with 4 grooves contains many tiny brownish seeds. Farewell-to-spring makes an attractive cut flower, which lasts for several days.

CULTURE

Farewell-to-spring can be grown in full sun to light shade. The soil should be moist but not wet until flowering starts, and then it can be quite dry. Warm, light, sandy loams are best, although heavier soils are tolerated if they are well drained. Do not apply additional fertilizer or the plants will become too tall and "leggy."

PROPAGATION

This hardy annual can be propagated only by seed, but it is easy and generally takes less than 90 days from seed to flowering plant. In coastal and hot desert regions seeds can be planted in the fall, but elsewhere they should be planted in the spring as soon as the soil starts to warm. Scratch the seeds into the soil surface in the desired location, and keep the soil moist until seeds germinate a week or two later. No chilling treatment is needed, but germination tends to be most rapid when the soil temperature is not excessively high. Thin seedlings to 6–9 inches apart.

COMPANIONS

Chinese houses, Douglas's wallflower, sky lupine, owl's clover, purple annual lupine, California poppy, California bluebell, checker bloom.

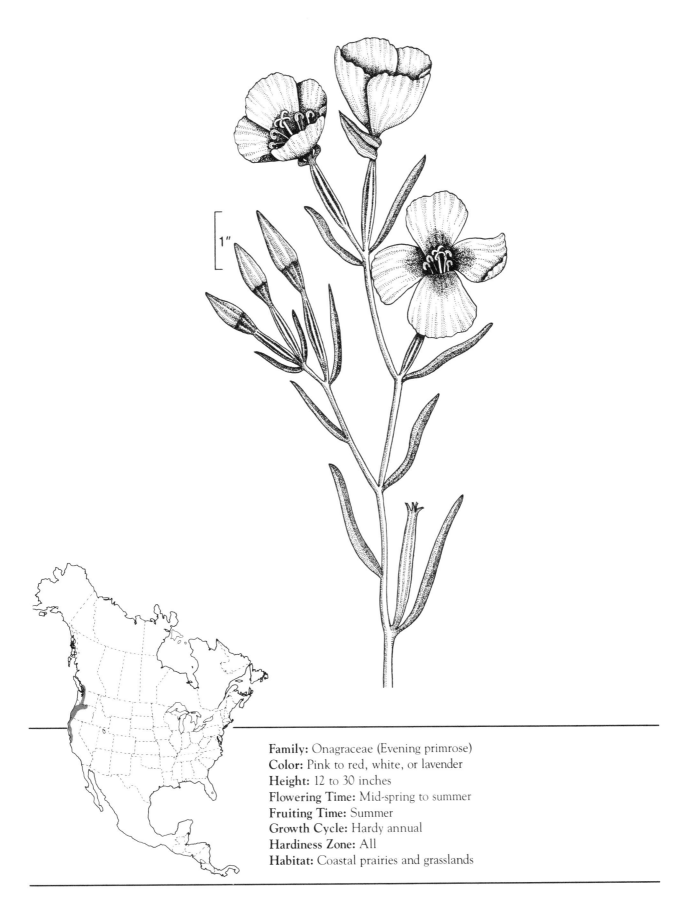

Family: Onagraceae (Evening primrose)
Color: Pink to red, white, or lavender
Height: 12 to 30 inches
Flowering Time: Mid-spring to summer
Fruiting Time: Summer
Growth Cycle: Hardy annual
Hardiness Zone: All
Habitat: Coastal prairies and grasslands

1"

FAREWELL-TO-SPRING *(Clarkia amoena)*

WESTERN SHOOTING STAR *Dodecatheon clevelandii*

(Padre's shooting star, *zarapico*)

Resembling miniature cyclamen with pointed centers, the western shooting stars burst forth in early spring in the meadows and open woodlands of California's Coastal Range. Linnaeus, the father of modern systematic botany, named the genus *Dodecatheon*, meaning "12 gods," because it was so beautiful it must be under the care of the dozen major classical deities. This species is also named in honor of the San Diego botanist Daniel Cleveland, who died in 1929. The smooth or slightly hairy, thick, pale green, 1½–3-inch-long leaves of the western shooting star form a rosette on the ground, out of which rises a 1–1½-foot-high scape bearing 2 to 16 spicy, fragrant flowers with 5 swept-back petals. The flowers, though usually pink, can range from nearly white to deep rose. The bases of the petals have white and yellow bands, and the 5 dark maroon anthers are fused into a tube surrounding the style. As the ½-inch capsular fruit matures and its many small (1/16-inch) seeds ripen, the leaves start to wither and by midsummer no trace of this lovely plant is left above ground. During its dormant period the plant recedes into its fibrous root system underground.

CULTURE Although the western shooting star grows well under a wide range of light conditions from full sun to shade, it prefers light shade. In the spring it needs moisture while its leaves and flowers are apparent, but when dormant this perennial is quite drought resistant and requires very little water. Rich, well-drained, but not excessively sandy soils, slightly acid to slightly alkaline (pH 6–7.5), are ideal. Western shooting star grows slowly, but is good for the rock garden.

PROPAGATION Western shooting star can be propagated by seed or root division. Plant the seeds 1/8–1/4 inch deep in flats, nursery beds, or permanent locations preferably in the fall, but if not then in the spring. Germination needs moisture, but no stratification. If using flats or nursery beds, keep the seedlings there until the end of the second year and then transplant them to the desired location. Since the aboveground foliage disappears during the summer, mark the locations of any mature plants you wish to divide while they are still visible. Divide the rootstocks in the fall, being sure that each piece has at least one bud. Plant the divisions 12–15 inches apart and ½ inches deep. The new divisions should be mulched if planted in regions with winter frost, but remove the mulch in the spring. Plants from divisions take several years to mature and flower, while plants from seed may take 4 or more years.

COMPANIONS Douglas's iris, tidy tips, Chinese houses, California poppy, checker bloom, coralbells.

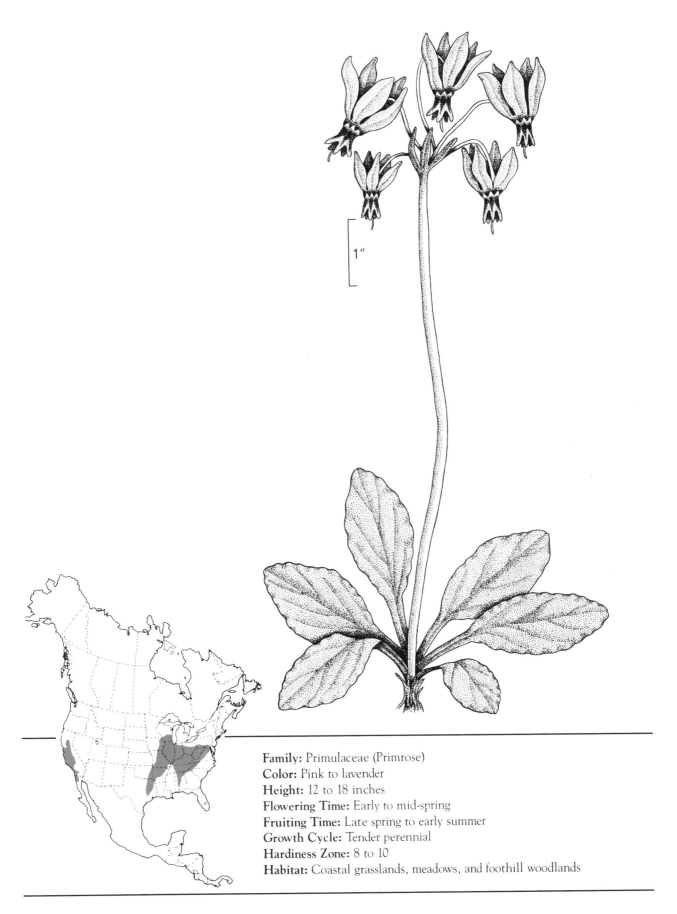

1"

Family: Primulaceae (Primrose)
Color: Pink to lavender
Height: 12 to 18 inches
Flowering Time: Early to mid-spring
Fruiting Time: Late spring to early summer
Growth Cycle: Tender perennial
Hardiness Zone: 8 to 10
Habitat: Coastal grasslands, meadows, and foothill woodlands

WESTERN SHOOTING STAR *(Dodecatheon clevelandii)*

CALIFORNIA POPPY

Eschscholzia californica

(Copa de oro, dormidera, amapola amarilla)

California should be known as the "Golden State" as much for its state flower, called *copa de oro* or "cup of gold" in Spanish, as for the Gold Rush of 1849. The California poppy has feathery, highly dissected, ¾–2½-inch-long, blue-green leaves, which clasp the 1–2-foot-high stems supporting single 1–3-inch-wide, 4-petaled flowers. The lustrous golden-orange petals open in the sunshine and close at night and on cloudy days, inspiring the Spanish common name *dormidera*, "the sleepy one." Flowers produced early in the spring tend to be larger than those produced later in the season. The flower color may be quite variable, ranging from deep orange to yellow, even for an individual plant over the growing season. A green, fused, caplike calyx or "calyptra" covers the bud and is thrust off as the petals expand. The spicy, fragrant flowers have a double-flanged disk below the petals, and at their centers are many stamens with linear anthers and a distinctive 4-part stigma. California poppy's 2–3-inch-long, 10-nerved, capsular fruit contains many 1/16-inch, gray-brown, roughened seeds. Long before this plant was introduced into European gardens in the 1830s, Native Americans used the watery juice of the roots as a pain killer for toothaches and ate the foliage as cooked greens.

CULTURE

California poppy is adaptable to almost any garden conditions as long as it has well-drained soils and plenty of sun. In its native range it flowers from late winter through late spring, and often again in the fall, but as a garden plant with enough water it can bloom all summer long. In hardiness zones 8–10 California poppy can be grown as a short-lived perennial, and in colder zones, as a hardy annual. It is excellent for naturalizing on sunny hillsides.

PROPAGATION

Plant the seeds in the fall directly where poppies are desired, since they do not transplant well. Sprinkle the seeds on the bare ground and gently rake them 1/8–1/4 inch deep with a garden rake, and water them until the rains come. The seeds will germinate in about 2 weeks without chilling treatment, and seedlings grow rapidly. Once established, California poppy will freely self-seed and may even become weedy — but what a beautiful weed!

COMPANIONS

Blue dicks, tidy tips, sky lupine, blue-eyed grass, baby blue-eyes, owl's clover, purple annual lupine.

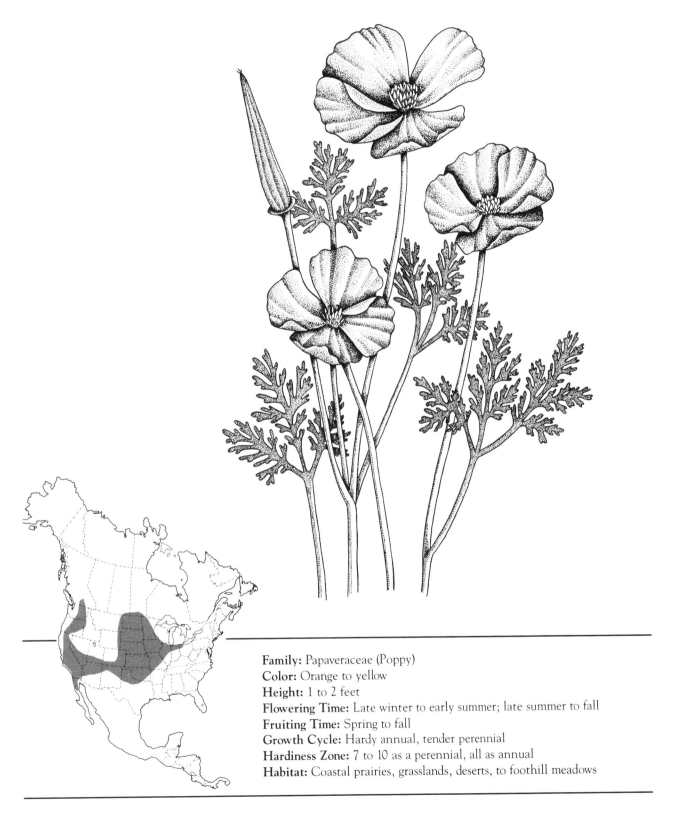

Family: Papaveraceae (Poppy)
Color: Orange to yellow
Height: 1 to 2 feet
Flowering Time: Late winter to early summer; late summer to fall
Fruiting Time: Spring to fall
Growth Cycle: Hardy annual, tender perennial
Hardiness Zone: 7 to 10 as a perennial, all as annual
Habitat: Coastal prairies, grasslands, deserts, to foothill meadows

CALIFORNIA POPPY *(Eschscholzia californica)*

DOUGLAS'S IRIS

Iris douglasiana

(Mountain iris, *lirio, flor de lis*)

Although the flowers of this West Coast native, popular in rock gardens, are usually blue, the colors can range from white to yellow to red-purple. The tufts of 6 or so 1–2-foot, sword-shaped, evergreen leaves arise from a short, stout, creeping rhizome. Frequently these tough yet flexible leaves have reddish bases. Several showy, 3–4-inch flowers, each with 3 downward-curving, petallike, 2-inch sepals, emerge from leafy bracts atop the 1–2-foot scape. The 3 petallike, 1½-inch style branches with crested stigmas lie against the sepals and surround the stamens. Each of the 3 narrow 2½-inch petals stands erect. Botanists have noted that a small proportion of the flowers have sterile stamens, and these individuals tend to flower and set fruit earlier in the season. Douglas's iris produces copious amounts of nectar, an ample reward for the bees and bumblebees that pollinate it. The ovary, tipped with nipple-like projections, develops into a 2-inch-long 3-sided capsule filled with rounded seeds.

CULTURE

In its native habitat in woods and meadows near the coast Douglas's iris starts to bloom in midwinter, and flowering progresses inland through the spring. While it can be grown in full sun, it prefers light shade and well-drained but moist, slightly acid (pH 5.5–6.5) soils rich in organic matter. It can tolerate a range of summer soil moisture conditions from drought to wet, but does not grow particularly well in alkaline soils. The tips of the leaves tend to turn brown in late spring and can be trimmed back during the summer. A tender perennial, Douglas's iris is difficult to grow in regions colder than hardiness zone 8. It is an excellent wildflower for shady banks and coastal gardens.

PROPAGATION

Propagate this species either by rhizome divisions or by seed. Divide rhizomes in the late fall or early spring by cutting the leaves back to about 5 inches and then cutting between the tufted clumps. Set the segments 6–12 inches apart with the leaf bases barely below the soil surface. The seeds of Douglas's iris require moist stratification (3 months at 40°F) and subsequent leaching by ground water to remove germination inhibitors. Plant fresh seeds in the early fall in a ¼–⅓-inch-deep layer of sphagnum moss in permanent locations, nursery beds, or flats that are left out over winter. Keep the seed bed moist and shaded. Germination typically takes place in January and February. Leave the seedlings in the holding beds or flats for the first season before transplanting them to permanent locations. It generally takes several years for seed-propagated plants to flower.

COMPANIONS

Western shooting star, blue-eyed grass, coralbells, checker bloom, Chinese houses.

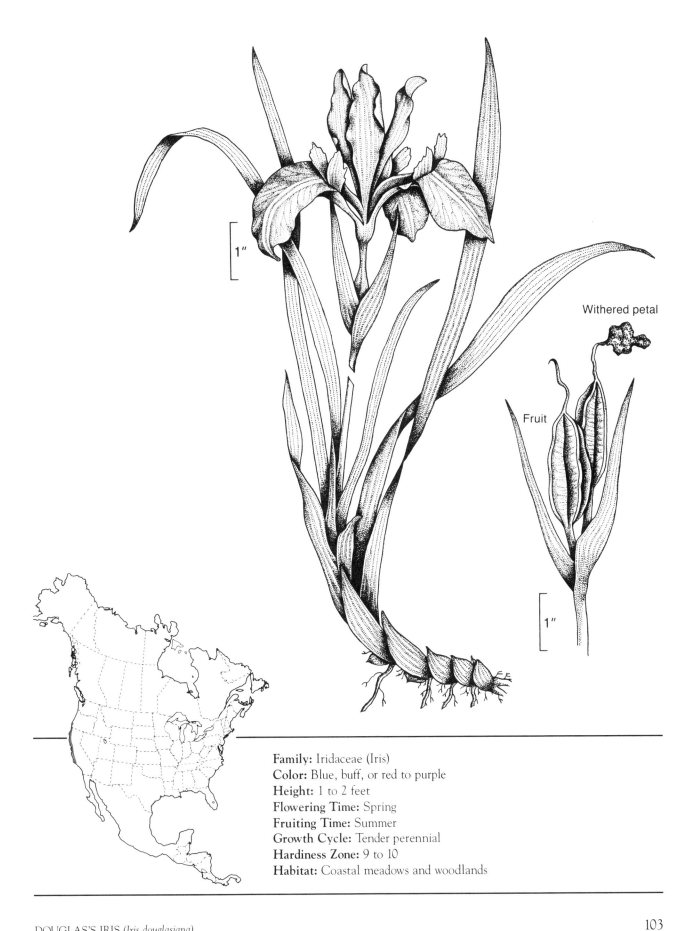

1"

Withered petal

Fruit

1"

Family: Iridaceae (Iris)
Color: Blue, buff, or red to purple
Height: 1 to 2 feet
Flowering Time: Spring
Fruiting Time: Summer
Growth Cycle: Tender perennial
Hardiness Zone: 9 to 10
Habitat: Coastal meadows and woodlands

DOUGLAS'S IRIS *(Iris douglasiana)*

GOLDFIELDS

Lasthenia californica
(L. chrysostoma, Baeria chrysostoma)

(Sunshine, baeria, coast goldfields, *brillo del sol*)

The prospectors in the Gold Rush didn't have to look very hard to find this small annual, for each spring it fills vast stretches of California grasslands with brilliant yellow *brillo del sol*, Spanish for "sunshine." The ½–1-inch-wide, yellow, daisy-like flower heads top 6-inch-high, sometimes branching stems. Each flower head has between 10 and 14 ¼–⅓-inch-long, bright yellow ray flowers surrounding the numerous, slightly darker disc flowers. The arrangement of ray flowers inspired the old Latin species name *chrysostoma*, which means "golden mouth." In its native habitat flies pollinate goldfields. Pairs of inch-long, grasslike, clasping leaves are scattered along the reddish stems, which, like the leaves, are sparsely covered with sharp, stiff hairs. The small, seedlike fruits of goldfields have 4 sides. Frequently goldfields is listed in seed catalogs by its old generic name, *Baeria*, honoring the Russian zoologist Karl Ernst von Baer. In the early 1800s goldfields seeds were sent from the Russian colony at Bodega Bay, California, to the Imperial Botanic Garden in St. Petersburg, Russia.

CULTURE

Goldfields is an annual of meadows and open woods and grows best in full sun to light shade. In dry, clayey soils goldfields is short and relatively unbranched, but in moister, richer soils it may reach nearly a foot in height and branches freely. When grown in hanging baskets it produces long sprays of lush green foliage and bright yellow flowers.

PROPAGATION

Goldfields is an annual and can be propagated only from seed. Plant the seeds ¼ inch deep where desired in the late fall in hardiness zones 9 and 10, where goldfields will germinate over the winter and quickly flower in the warmth of spring. In other regions it should be grown as a spring annual planted as soon as the soil can be worked. Once established goldfields self-seeds freely in its native range, although elsewhere it is advisable to collect the seed as it matures and save it for planting the following spring.

COMPANIONS

Tidy tips, California poppy, baby blue-eyes, wind poppy, owl's clover, California bluebells.

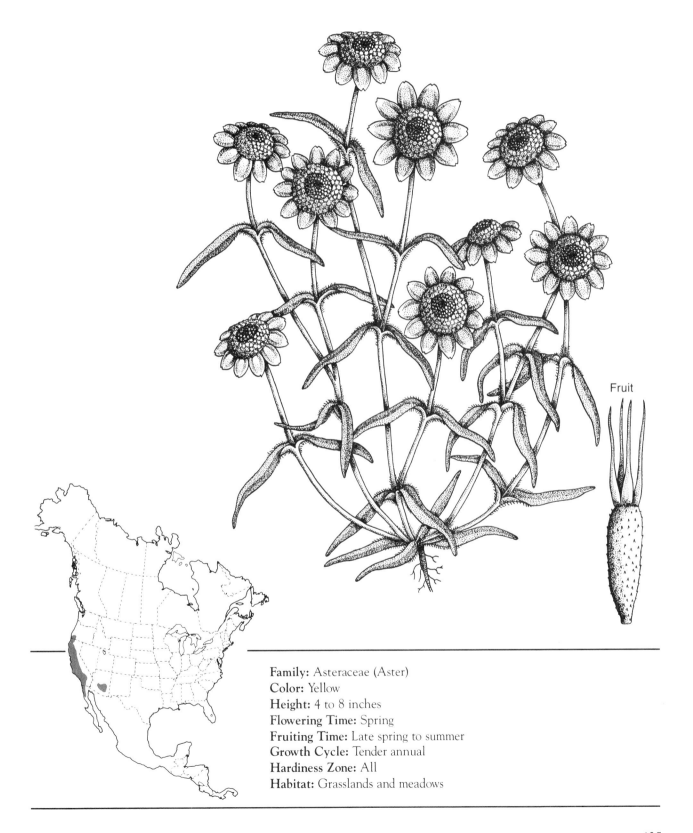

Fruit

Family: Asteraceae (Aster)
Color: Yellow
Height: 4 to 8 inches
Flowering Time: Spring
Fruiting Time: Late spring to summer
Growth Cycle: Tender annual
Hardiness Zone: All
Habitat: Grasslands and meadows

GOLDFIELDS (*Lasthenia californica*)

TIDY TIPS
Layia platyglossa

(Coastal tidy tips)

The tips of this member of the aster family are not actually tidier than those of other composite species, but the plant does have ray flowers with white, 3-toothed petal tips, contrasting with deep yellow petal bases. Tidy tips stands 4–16 inches high with fragrant 1–1½-inch-wide flower heads atop sprawling, branched stems. While most of the ray flowers have white and yellow petals, some individuals are all white or all yellow. The disc flowers in the center of the flower heads are yellow with long black anthers that project beyond the tubular petals and provide an interesting contrast to the ray flowers. Tufted, 1/8-inch-long, dandelion-seed-like fruits are produced by both ray and disc flowers and are released by the summer breezes. Both the stems and the scattered, ½-inch-long leaves are densely hairy.

CULTURE   Grow tidy tips in the full sun. Although it is quite adaptable to a variety of garden soils, it does best in sandy loams. The soil should be slightly moist while the seedlings are growing rapidly in the early spring, but thereafter it should be on the dry side since tidy tips does not grow well under excessively wet conditions. This annual is excellent for naturalizing on well-drained sites with poor soils, especially if mixed with other annuals and native bunch grasses. Tidy tips can be an elegant garden plant, as European gardeners found out after its introduction in the 1880s, and creates a spectacular effect if planted thickly in beds.

PROPAGATION   Sow seeds in the late fall or early spring. No chilling treatment of the seed is needed and in regions colder than hardiness zone 9, tidy tips can easily be started indoors in the late winter. Plant the seeds 1/8–1/4 inch deep in sandy soil and keep moist until germination takes place 1 to 2 weeks later. Seedlings will grow rapidly and produce flowers in about 60 days. Flowering may continue into the summer.

COMPANIONS   Goldfields, baby blue-eyes, California poppy, farewell-to-spring, owl's clover, sky lupine, and many other West Coast annuals.

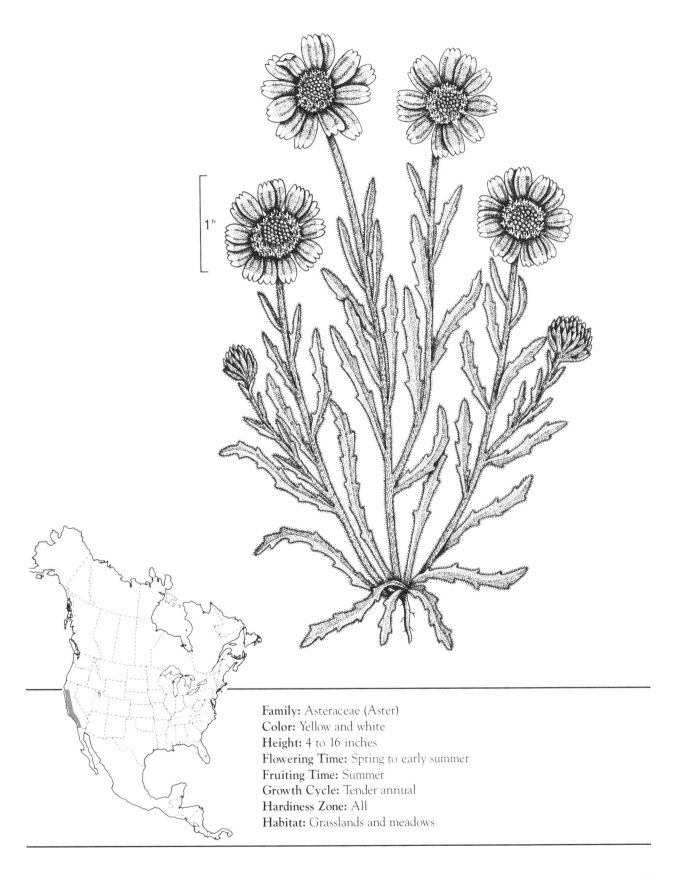

1"

Family: Asteraceae (Aster)
Color: Yellow and white
Height: 4 to 16 inches
Flowering Time: Spring to early summer
Fruiting Time: Summer
Growth Cycle: Tender annual
Hardiness Zone: All
Habitat: Grasslands and meadows

TIDY TIPS *(Layia platyglossa)*

PURPLE ANNUAL LUPINE

Lupinus succulentus

(Arroyo lupine, succulent lupine, *lupino, altramuz*)

With the growing disturbance of the Southern California landscape, this lovely annual has increasingly become a weedy roadside plant. Purple annual lupine is also abundant immediately following fires in the coastal sage scrub of its native range. The succulent, fleshy, 8–24-inch stems have 7 to 9 dark green, smooth, round-tipped, 2–3-inch leaflets making up the palmately compound leaves. A small organ known as the pulvinus at the base of each leaflet senses the direction of the sun and adjusts the leaf's position to track the sun from east to west during the daylight hours. Clusters of deep purple to dark blue to rusty red blooms are borne at the tops of the stems. Each of the ½-inch-long flowers is a solid color except for the uppermost banner petal, which has a yellow center. Honeybees are the major pollinator of the purple annual lupine. The 2-inch-long pod-fruits have 8 to 10 brown, mottled, ¼-inch-long seeds.

CULTURE

Purple annual lupine is the most easily grown native lupine and is quite adaptable to garden conditions. It should be grown in full sun on dry, well-drained soils. Keep the soil moist as the seeds are germinating and the seedlings are becoming established, but don't overwater or mildew diseases of the leaves may result. If you need to inoculate purple annual lupine to establish it in your soil, use *Lupinus* rhizobia (Nitragin-type Lupinus special #5). Snails enjoy eating the young seedlings and may need to be controlled if they are overly abundant.

PROPAGATION

Like many other legume seeds, purple annual lupine has enhanced germination following scarification, or nicking of the seed coat. Rub the seeds between two sheets of medium-grit sandpaper and allow the seeds to soak overnight in warm water before planting at a depth of $1/8–1/4$ inch. Plant seeds in the fall in hardiness zones 9 and 10, and in the early spring elsewhere. If you start the seeds indoors in the early spring, transplant the seedlings to desired locations before they get too large, or establishment may be difficult. Thin seedlings to 6–8 inches apart.

COMPANIONS

California poppy, sky lupine, wind poppy, golden yarrow, Douglas's wallflower, blazing star, and other West Coast annuals.

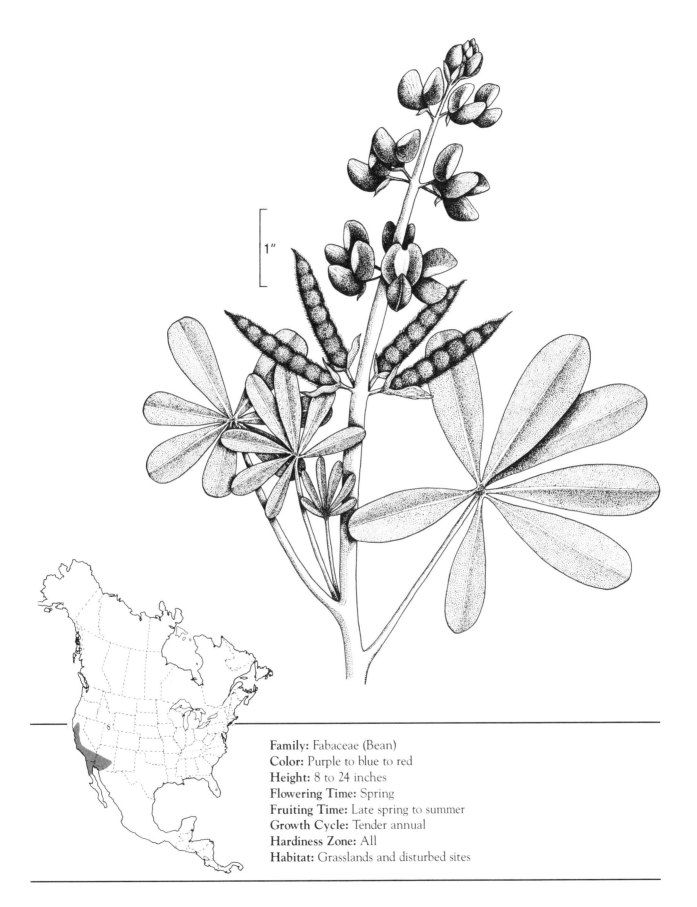

1"

Family: Fabaceae (Bean)
Color: Purple to blue to red
Height: 8 to 24 inches
Flowering Time: Spring
Fruiting Time: Late spring to summer
Growth Cycle: Tender annual
Hardiness Zone: All
Habitat: Grasslands and disturbed sites

PURPLE ANNUAL LUPINE *(Lupinus succulentus)*

OWL'S CLOVER
Orthocarpus purpurascens

(Pink paint brush, *escobita*)

The small flowers of this sometimes parasitic relative of the snapdragon resemble the heads of owls, hence the English common name. The Spanish common name translates to "little broom," describing the upright tufts of flowers and bracts that cover the top of the stem. The stem is 4–16 inches high and densely covered with ascending, threadlike, ½–2-inch leaves and masses of ½–¾-inch rose and yellow or rose and white flowers. A desert variety of this species has more deeply pigmented flowers. The upper lip of the flower is formed by the fusion of 2 petals into a velvety rose-purple beak and projects over the swollen, lighter-hued, 3-lobed lower lip dotted with yellow or purple. While each flower has stamens and a pistil with a large stigma, insects must bring pollen from different plants in order for it to produce seeds. Below each of the flowers is a 5- to 7-lobed bright crimson or purple bract. The fruit is a ½-inch-long capsule filled with very small seeds. A plant of southwestern grasslands, owl's clover is frequently parasitic on the roots of grasses, from which it obtains some of its nourishment.

CULTURE

Although owl's clover is usually a parasitic plant in its native range, it can be easily cultivated in garden habitats without providing host grass plants if it is grown with other wildflowers. Even in the wild, owl's clover does not require the presence of host grasses in order to germinate and establish itself. Grow owl's clover in full sun on well-drained soils — sandy soils that are moist in the spring are ideal. Once flowering has started, the soils can be allowed to become drier.

PROPAGATION

Propagate owl's clover by seed, with no chilling treatment. Scratch the seeds into the soil in the desired location in early fall and keep moist while they germinate and establish seedlings. They typically germinate when soil temperatures are near 80°F.

COMPANIONS

Goldfields, tidy tips, sky lupine, wind poppy, annual purple lupine, California bluebell, California poppy.

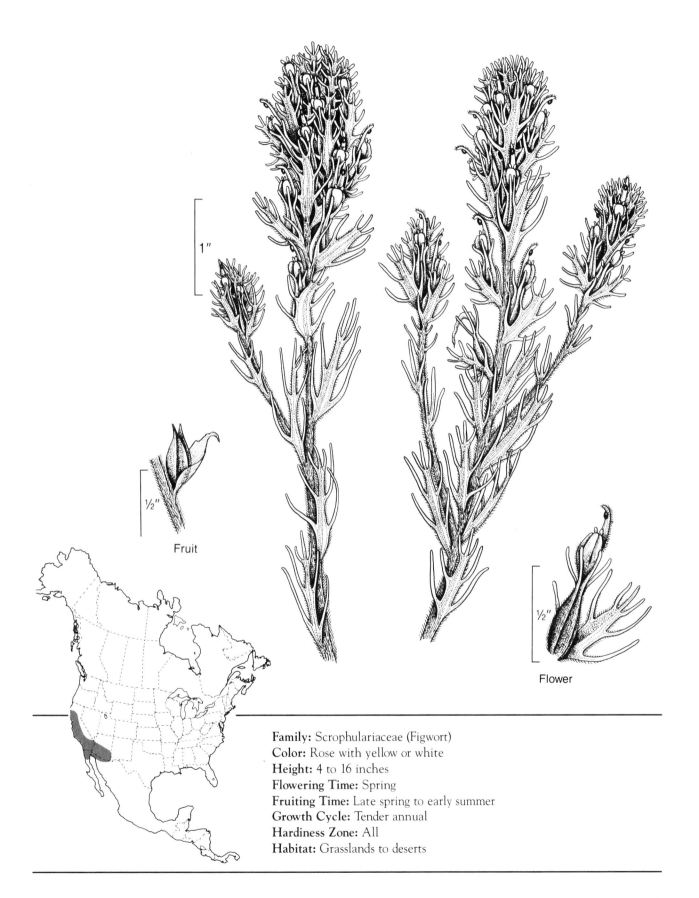

1"

½"

Fruit

½"

Flower

Family: Scrophulariaceae (Figwort)
Color: Rose with yellow or white
Height: 4 to 16 inches
Flowering Time: Spring
Fruiting Time: Late spring to early summer
Growth Cycle: Tender annual
Hardiness Zone: All
Habitat: Grasslands to deserts

OWL'S CLOVER *(Orthocarpus purpurascens)*

CHECKER BLOOM
Sidalcea malvaeflora

(Wild hollyhock, checker mallow)

Checker bloom produces miniature pink hollyhocks in the late winter and spring-time along the Pacific Coast and on the low elevations of inland California. This perennial has somewhat fleshy, slightly fuzzy, 1–2-inch-broad leaves with long stalks that emerge in a clump from the extensive, thick, woody root. The first leaves to appear are round and geranium-like with pie crust edges, but the later leaves, scattered along the semi-erect stems, are more deeply cut, like a bird's foot with 5 to 7 toes. The stems eventually reach 8–12 inches in height and bear up to a dozen or so inch-long flowers that open from the bottom toward the top over a 4 to 6 week period. The lavender to pink flowers, which open with the morning sun and twist closed at night, have raised white veins on their 5 petals and are joined at the base. The many stamens are fused together in 2 rings, forming a column in the center of the flower. Three to ten anthers, which turn rose-pink as they mature, are situated inside the stamen column, and the elongated style and stigmas grow outward through the anthers. As the fruit matures, the ovaries separate into flattened, 1/8-inch-wide seeds. Checker bloom has many varied sub-species distinguished by differences in growth form, leaf shape, degree of hairiness, and seed size.

CULTURE   Grow checker bloom in full sun to light shade on soils that are well drained but not excessively so. The soil should be kept moist during the winter and the spring flowering season, and then can be allowed to become drier. After the fruits have matured in the summer the dead shoots can be cut back to the ground. Checker bloom has long been a favorite of rock gardeners, even in England.

PROPAGATION   Checker bloom is most easily propagated from seed planted in the late fall. Germination is enhanced if seeds are soaked in hot water overnight. Then plant the seeds the next morning about ¼ inch deep and keep the soil moist, but not wet, until the seedlings appear. In its native range, checker bloom self-seeds easily. Some plants from fall sowings produce flowers the first year and the remainder will bloom the following spring. If given the proper conditions checker bloom will start to spread after several years. You can also propagate checker bloom by dividing the root crowns in the winter before the flowering stem starts to develop. Cut the root lengthwise into 2 to 3 pieces, each with several leaves and buds, and replant the cuttings 8–12 inches apart with the buds just at the ground level.

COMPANIONS   Douglas's iris, farewell-to-spring, linanthus, showy penstemon, sky lupine.

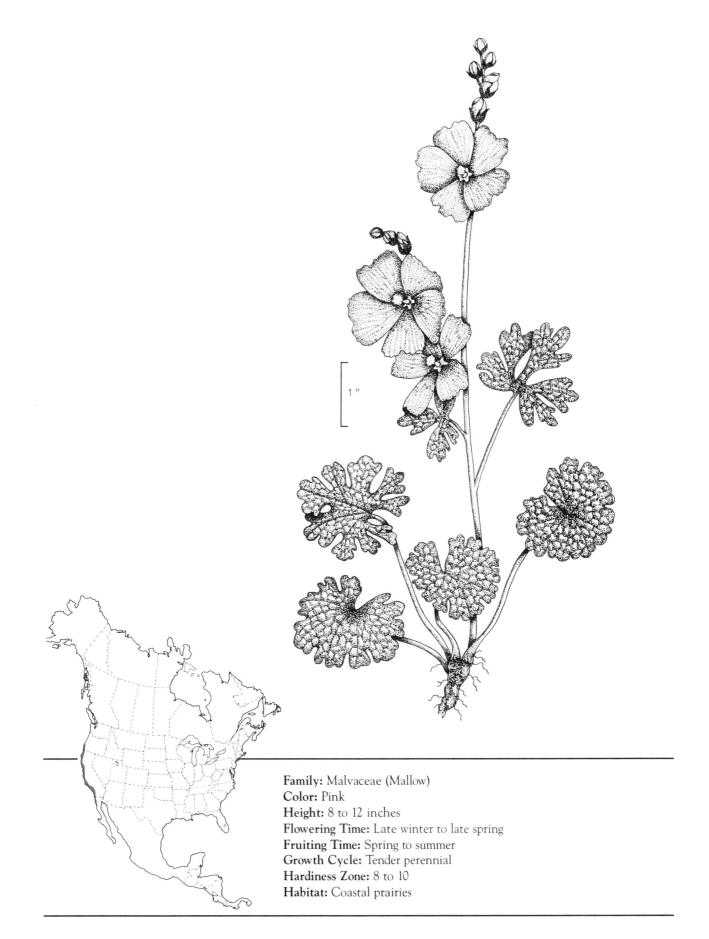

1 "

Family: Malvaceae (Mallow)
Color: Pink
Height: 8 to 12 inches
Flowering Time: Late winter to late spring
Fruiting Time: Spring to summer
Growth Cycle: Tender perennial
Hardiness Zone: 8 to 10
Habitat: Coastal prairies

CHECKER BLOOM *(Sidalcea malvaeflora)*

BLUE-EYED GRASS

Sisyrinchium bellum

(Western blue-eyed grass, *azulea*, *purole*)

The scientific name of this native perennial means "beautiful Sisyrinchium," and beautiful it is. Though a member of the iris family, its flowers don't look much like those of Douglas's iris (page 102). Blue-eyed grass has small, saucer-shaped, purple-blue to lilac flowers with 3 petals and 3 identical petallike sepals enclosed by a pair of bracts. The petals, which open with the sun and close at night and in cloudy weather, have blunt tips with a projecting point. At the golden center of the flower are 3 stamens and a stigma that becomes 3-clefted after fertilization. Each of the inch-wide flowers is relatively short-lived, but since they are in clusters of 4 to 7, the spring flowering season is fairly long. A round capsule develops in the early summer and contains a few black, 1/8-inch seeds. The foliage of blue-eyed grass looks like 4–16-inch-high clumps of grass, and without flowers present, one might easily mistake this plant for grass. In addition, the branched stems, which are slightly taller than the leaves, are flattened, resembling grass stems. Fibrous roots of blue-eyed grass spread vigorously with time, forming dense colonies.

CULTURE

Blue-eyed grass grows naturally in coastal meadows and around vernal pools that hold water in late winter and spring but dry up by early summer. It can also be found growing in open oak woodlands and even along with sagebrush. While it is flowering, this species benefits from temporarily wet soils, but the soils should be allowed to dry out during the summer. As long as blue-eyed grass is grown in the full sun and the soils are dry in the summer, it can be grown on any kind of soil ranging from sands to loams to clays. There are a number of subspecies and varieties of blue-eyed grass, and some can be grown as annuals to hardiness zone 6. The plants can be successfully grown in pots that are left out in the spring, given little water during the summer, and brought indoors over winter. In winter, they should be kept moist but not wet. Blue-eyed grass is also attractive in a rock garden or planted around the bases of shrubs and trees.

PROPAGATION

Blue-eyed grass can be propagated by root divisions or by seed. Divide the clumps early in the spring just as the grasslike foliage is emerging. Set the bases of the shoots ¼–½ inch deep and tamp the soil to secure good root contact. Plant the seeds ¼ inch deep in the desired locations in the late summer or early fall. The seeds do not require stratification or other treatment. Germination will take place by the early spring, and plants from seed will usually flower the second year. No thinning is needed.

COMPANIONS

Blue dicks, California poppy, blazing star, owl's clover, tidy tips, goldfields.

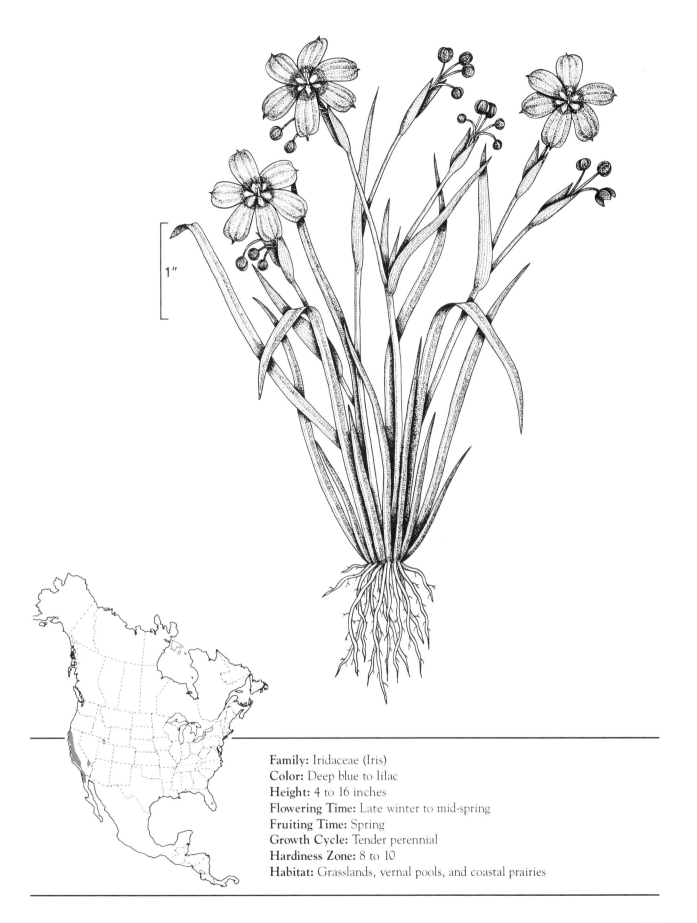

Family: Iridaceae (Iris)
Color: Deep blue to lilac
Height: 4 to 16 inches
Flowering Time: Late winter to mid-spring
Fruiting Time: Spring
Growth Cycle: Tender perennial
Hardiness Zone: 8 to 10
Habitat: Grasslands, vernal pools, and coastal prairies

BLUE-EYED GRASS *(Sisyrinchium bellum)*

WIND POPPY

Stylomecon heterophylla

(Flaming poppy, blood drop)

The flaming red-orange flowers of the wind poppy are borne on 1–2-foot-high stems that sway in the spring breezes of western California. The 1–2-inch-wide flowers have 4 broad, silky, vermilion petals with dark purple spots at their bases. Flowers of plants from the southern part of wind poppy's range are usually smaller than those in central California. In the center of the flower are many purple filaments, each with a bright yellow anther. The stamens encircle an elongated style and a round, 4-to-8-lobed, yellow, caplike stigma. The stem and the 1–6-inch-long, deeply cleft, round-lobed leaves exude a yellow sap. Leaves are denser near the ground, and the long flowering stem with its single nodding bud rises from a rosette of leaves. As the flower bud opens, it becomes erect and the 2 sepals that covered the tightly compacted petals open and fall off. The blooms are quite fragile and therefore don't make particularly good cut flowers. The ½-inch-long capsule fruit of the wind poppy has an unusual shape, like a ribbed toy top, with 8 pores at the top through which the small seeds are dispersed. Frequently wind poppy can be found invading fields soon after fires.

CULTURE
Wind poppy can be grown in a range of light conditions from full sun to shade, but do best in locations that are sunny part of the day and shady for at least several hours. The soil should be moderately moist, and good drainage is more important than whether the soil is light or heavy. This annual does very well under normal garden conditions, especially in shady borders and at the edges of woodlands.

PROPAGATION
The only way to propagate wind poppy is by seed. Scratch the seeds lightly into the surface of the soil, and keep moist but not wet until the flowering period has passed. Seeds should be planted in the fall in wind poppy's native range in hardiness zones 9 and 10, and in the spring elsewhere. You can start the seedlings in peat pots indoors in late winter and transplant the entire pot, after removing the bottom, to the desired location. In its native range wind poppy will self-seed, forming spectacular clumps of plants in the garden.

COMPANIONS
Chinese houses, coralbells, purple annual lupine, baby blue-eyes, Douglas's iris, showy penstemon, California poppy, Douglas's wallflower.

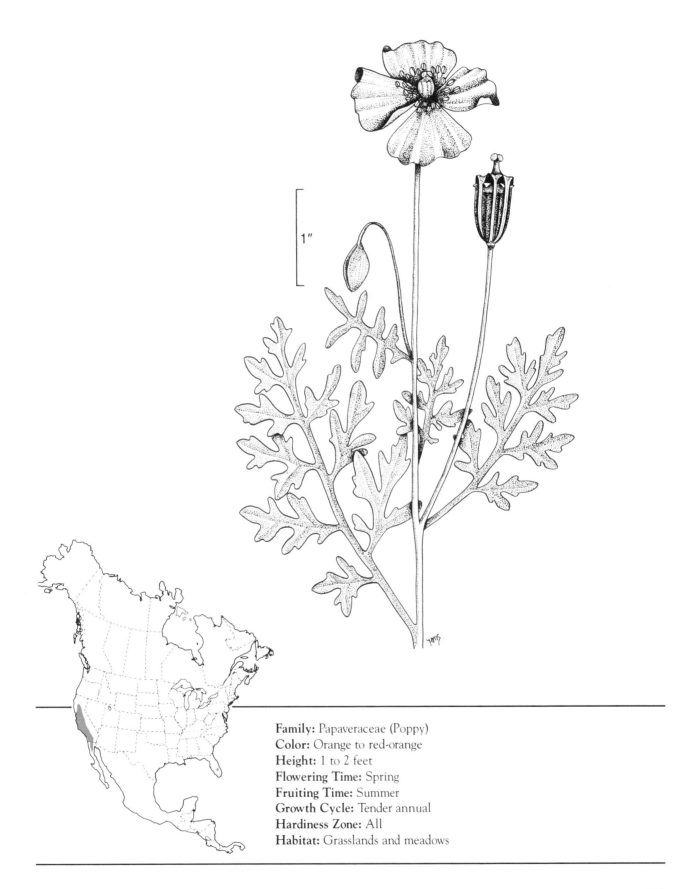

Family: Papaveraceae (Poppy)
Color: Orange to red-orange
Height: 1 to 2 feet
Flowering Time: Spring
Fruiting Time: Summer
Growth Cycle: Tender annual
Hardiness Zone: All
Habitat: Grasslands and meadows

WIND POPPY *(Stylomecon heterophylla)*

CHAPARRAL SPECIES

Chaparral plants are highly adapted to survive both drought and fire. They grow where the winters are wet and the summers are hot and dry. Chaparral soils are often gravelly and excessively drained and support plants that are deeply rooted or can manage on little water during the dry season. The species presented in this section generally make excellent rock garden plants and can be used for erosion control as well. While some chaparral plants are highly flammable, others are more fire-retardant or reduce fire danger through their low-growth forms. In planning a chaparral garden, take advantage of native plants that reduce both water consumption and the chance of fire damage to your property (see sections dealing with xeriscaping on page 18 and with fire-scaping on page 19).

Even though the environmental conditions of chaparral tend to be extreme, there are many choices of companions for those native plants presented here. If your garden is small, choose low-growing perennials such as **California peony** (*Paeonia californica*) or **prickly phlox** (*Leptodactylon californicum*). California peony has inch-wide, hanging, maroon and red flowers atop fleshy 6–18-inch-high stems. The foliage is an attractive blue-green during the spring growing season. Prickly phlox is a 1–3-foot-high, semi-woody species that is easy to grow and will both self-seed and spread with time. Its bright pink to rose phloxlike flowers are in soft contrast to its rather stiff, gray-green, needlelike foliage.

If parts of your garden are moist and partially shaded, you might consider **canyon sunflower** (*Venegasia carpesioides*) or the low shrub **bush monkey flower** (*Mimulus longiflorus*). Canyon sunflower is a 1–3-foot-high perennial with attractive 4-inch-long triangular leaves and showy, yellow, 3-inch-wide sunflower heads arising from the axils of the upper leaves. The bush monkey flower grows 1–3 feet high and has masses of puffy, salmon to peach-orange blossoms from spring through most of the summer. Several horticultural varieties are available and sometimes are listed in the trade as *Diplacus longiflorus*.

Of the numerous **California lilac** (*Ceanothus*) species and horticultural varieties to choose for intermediate to large chaparral gardens, *Ceanothus thyrsiflorus* or **blue blossom ceanothus** is one of the most appealing. This relatively hardy shrub grows 6–20 feet high and about as wide. Its 3-inch spikes of light to dark

Chaparral garden

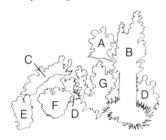

A. Prickly poppy
B. Our Lord's candle
C. California fuchsia
D. Blue dicks
E. Douglas's wallflower
F. Golden yarrow
G. Showy penstemon

blue flowers are present only in the spring, but its glossy, dark green leaves are attractive throughout the year. There are also many species of **manzanita** (*Arctostaphylos*) to consider. Manzanitas are slow-growing evergreen shrubs with year-round appeal. In the spring they bear attractive clusters of white to pink flowers that in time mature into tiny, apple-like fruit, as the Spanish common name ("little apple") indicates. Birds find the bright red fruits irresistible. Both the **common manzanita** (*Arctostaphylos manzanita*), which grows to 20 feet, and the smaller, pink-flowered *Arctostaphylos bakeri*, which grows 5–6 feet high, have gnarled maroon bark and crooked branches.

Large, showy, bright yellow flowers and lobed, fuzzy, persistent green and tan leaves make the **flannel bush** (*Fremontodendron californicum*) one of the most beautiful chaparral shrubs. It grows 6–20 feet high and about as wide. Flannel bush is ideal for xeriscaping, and additional water should be avoided during the dry season because this species is susceptible to root rot. Either purchase nursery-propagated stock or raise it from moist, stratified seeds. **Fuchsia-flowered gooseberry** (*Ribes speciosum*) is a deciduous shrub that grows to 6 feet, with arching, thorny branches. In late winter its leaves reappear and it bears inch-long bright red fuchsia-like flowers that dangle in rows from the ends of the branches.

PRICKLY POPPY

Argemone munita

(*Cardo santo, chicalote, mindri*)

Ranchers might think it odd to include in this book a poisonous "weed" that invades dry rangelands and roadsides, yet it is a beautiful and adaptable wildflower, truly a *cardo santo*, or "blessed thistle." Prickly poppy is at home in the Colorado and Mojave Deserts as well as in the mountains of Southern California at elevations from 1500 to 5000 feet. A sticky yellow sap oozes from wounds in the 1–3-foot, sometimes purplish, branched stems and their clasping, lobed leaves. This sap contains an alkaloid, isoquinolin, which is toxic when consumed by humans and range animals, and gives the plant insecticidal protection as well. The fierce spines on the foliage and stems, however, make it unlikely to be eaten. The many showy flowers, each borne at the tip of a branch, are reason enough for including this plant in the garden, rather than leaving it in its home on the range. Although the flower buds and sepals are spiny, the 6 white petals of the 2–5-inch flowers have the texture of crepe paper. In the center of the flower, numerous yellow stamens surround the pistil with its brown-purple, scallop-edged stigma. The fruit, a bristly capsule, contains many small ($1/16$-inch) seeds which, at maturity, shake out through holes in the top as it sways in the wind.

CULTURE

Prickly poppy, an extremely drought-tolerant, short-lived perennial, is best grown on dry, sandy to gravelly soils in full sun. It will grow well on better soils, as long as they are well drained, and is well adapted to gardens nearly anywhere. Prickly poppy is quite resistant to insect pests, and those that visit it do little harm.

PROPAGATION

Propagate prickly poppy from seed. This plant grows as an annual or perennial, depending on its variety and growing conditions, but it flowers the first year from seed regardless. No cold treatment of the seeds is needed; in fact, germination is often enhanced when they are scorched by fire (see page 49). Plant the fire-treated seeds and charate in the late autumn $1/8$ inch deep where desired. In regions with short growing seasons, start seeds in flats or pots indoors in the early spring and transplant to permanent locations when the seedlings are robust. Be careful when transplanting, especially if the seedlings have been raised in flats, because the root systems are quite fragile. Once established, prickly poppy may self-seed.

COMPANIONS

Douglas's wallflower, blue dicks, desert marigold, desert sand verbena, showy penstemon, southwestern verbena.

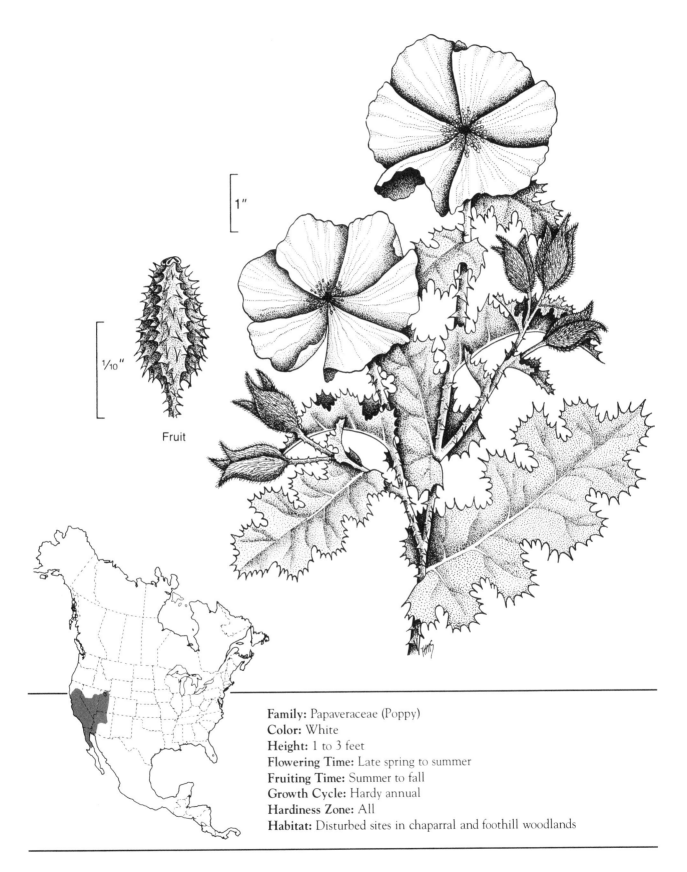

1"

1/10"

Fruit

Family: Papaveraceae (Poppy)
Color: White
Height: 1 to 3 feet
Flowering Time: Late spring to summer
Fruiting Time: Summer to fall
Growth Cycle: Hardy annual
Hardiness Zone: All
Habitat: Disturbed sites in chaparral and foothill woodlands

PRICKLY POPPY (*Argemone munita*)

BLUE DICKS

Brodiaea pulchella
(*Dichelostemma pulchellum, D. capitatum*)

(Wild hyacinth, wild potato, *cacomite, coquito de tierra*)

Blue dicks is a spring-flowering perennial common on coastal plains and dry low-lands in California. Grasslike, 6–16-inch-long leaves and a smooth, round, 2–3-foot stem arise from a scaly corm. These corms were eaten both raw and cooked by Native Americans, inspiring the common names "wild potato" and *coquito de tierra* or "fruit of the earth." Up to a dozen violet-blue, ½–¾-inch flowers cluster tightly in a roundish head at the top of the scape, just above several short leafy bracts, sometimes purple. The bases of the 6 petals are fused together to form a ball-like tube. Blue dicks blooms from March to May and makes an excellent, long-lasting cut flower. Its fruits are ¼-inch-long capsules containing many 1/8-inch seeds. After the fruits have matured in early summer, the leaves wither, and the plant enters dormancy until the following spring.

CULTURE
Blue dicks thrives in poor, dry soils in sunny locations. It tolerates drought and is ideal for sunny banks and locations that are droughty in the summer. In its native habitat, this half-hardy perennial is frequently found growing on heavy, gritty clay soils. As long as the soil is well drained, however, blue dicks is adaptable to normal moisture conditions. If moisture-related problems such as root rot occur, cover the surface of the soil above the dormant corms with plastic sheeting or panes of glass. Although blue dicks does well in hardiness zone 9 and warmer regions, it should be heavily mulched in hardiness zones 7 and 8. In colder regions the corms should be dug up for the winter and stored in a cool, dry place.

PROPAGATION
Blue dicks can be propagated easily by seed or corm divisions. The seed requires no treatment for germination. Plant seeds ¼ inch deep in a sandy loam, and keep them moist but not wet. If seeds are sown in permanent locations, the plants should be thinned to 3–5 inches apart by digging up the dormant cormlets and spacing them properly. If flats or nursery beds are used, transplant the dormant cormlets with the same spacing, 2–2½ inches deep. Plants from seed require 2 to 3 years to flower. Every few years, dig up the mature corms in the fall and carefully divide the offset corms. Plant the divided corms 3–5 inches apart and 3–4 inches deep.

COMPANIONS
Golden yarrow, California poppy, blue-eyed grass, showy penstemon, California bluebells, prickly poppy.

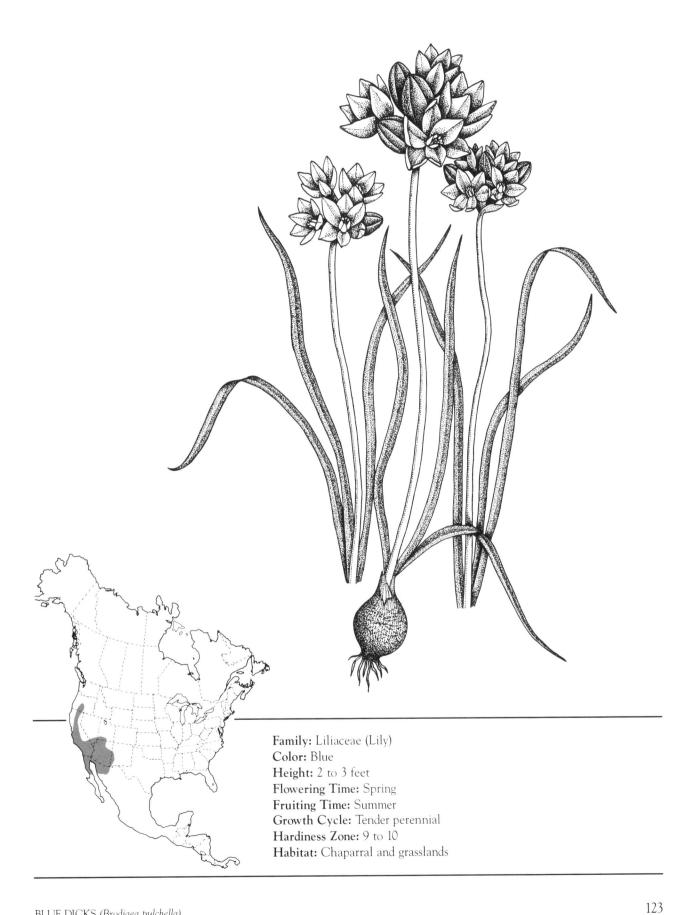

Family: Liliaceae (Lily)
Color: Blue
Height: 2 to 3 feet
Flowering Time: Spring
Fruiting Time: Summer
Growth Cycle: Tender perennial
Hardiness Zone: 9 to 10
Habitat: Chaparral and grasslands

BLUE DICKS *(Brodiaea pulchella)*

GOLDEN YARROW   *Eriophyllum confertiflorum*

(Long-stemmed eriophyllum, yellow yarrow)

The English translation of the scientific generic name *Eriophyllum* is "woolly leaf." The woolly fuzz that densely covers the leaves and stems of this southwestern California perennial was collected by Native Americans and used as a cure for rheumatism. Its several 1–2-foot-high, erect, herbaceous stems arise from a woody base. The erect, clasping, gray-green, 1–1½-inch-long leaves are dissected somewhat like the leaves of garden tansy, with edges that curl toward their densely woolly undersides. The leaves are more numerous toward the base of the stem. At the top of the stem are dense, flat-topped clusters of bright golden-yellow yarrowlike flower heads, inspiring the name *confertiflorum*, which means "crowded flower" in Latin. The flower heads, only ½ inch across, are massed into clusters several inches in diameter. Golden yarrow is not really a yarrow, but a member of the aster family. The 4 to 6 ray flowers have ¼-inch-long round-tipped petals and surround the several disc flowers in the center of the head. Golden yarrow's 1/8-inch seed-like fruit has distinct sides.

CULTURE

Plant golden yarrow in dry, well-drained soils in sunny locations. The most important aspect of successfully growing this perennial is not over-irrigating when temperatures are cool. Golden yarrow withstands the summer heat and droughty conditions in the Coastal Ranges and Sierra Nevada foothills very well. In the more humid regions of northern California the soils may require the addition of coarse sand or gravel. This tender perennial can be grown in hardiness zones 9 and 10, but in zone 8 a heavy mulch is needed in winter and should be removed in the spring. In colder regions, growing this plant is chancy, even with a heavy mulch, unless you want to grow it in a large pot and bring it indoors over the winter.

PROPAGATION

Even though golden yarrow is a perennial, its woody stem base and root crown make propagation by division difficult. It is easily propagated by seeds, however, which require no chilling treatment. Plant the seeds in the fall ¼ inch deep, keeping the soil moist until the seedlings become established. Heating the seeds (bake at 250°F for 5 minutes) before planting, and strewing a thin layer of charred plant remains on the surface of the soil following planting, may enhance germination. Sow seeds where the plants are desired since golden yarrow is difficult to transplant.

COMPANIONS

Showy penstemon, Douglas's wallflower, prickly poppy, blue dicks, Indian pink.

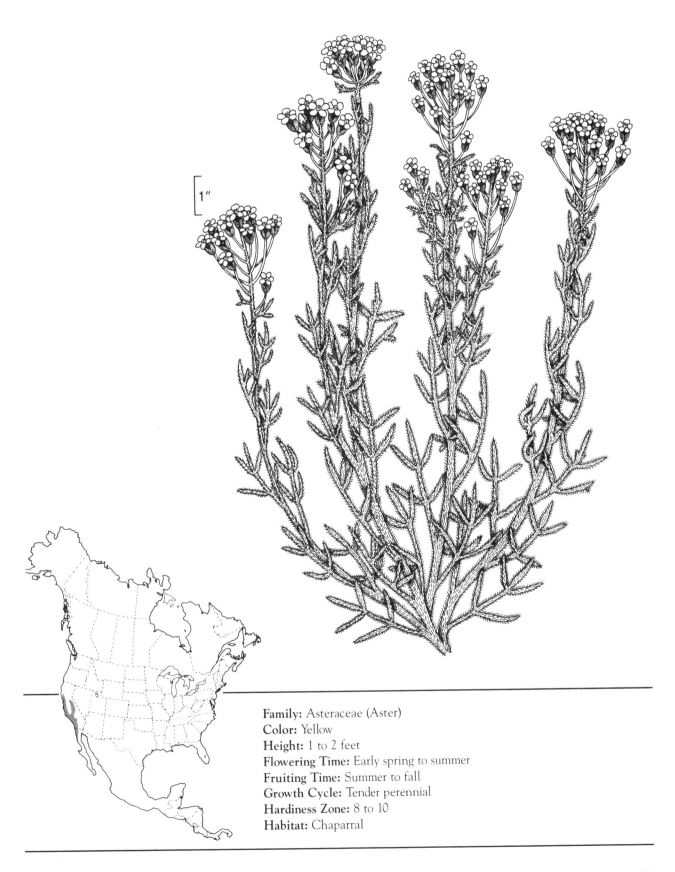

Family: Asteraceae (Aster)
Color: Yellow
Height: 1 to 2 feet
Flowering Time: Early spring to summer
Fruiting Time: Summer to fall
Growth Cycle: Tender perennial
Hardiness Zone: 8 to 10
Habitat: Chaparral

GOLDEN YARROW (*Eriophyllum confertiflorum*)

DOUGLAS'S WALLFLOWER

Erysimum capitatum
(E. arkansanum)

(Coast wallflower, western wallflower, *alheli*)

The light burnt orange color of Douglas's wallflower makes it one of the loveliest plants in this collection, and even its rarer yellow, brick red, or maroon forms are most appealing. The erect 1–3-foot-high stems bear 1–5-inch-long, slender, lance-shaped leaves with small teeth on their edges. Both the leaves, which are largest and densest near the ground, and the stems are covered with gray hairs. Atop the stem are oval clusters of fragrant, ¾–1-inch-wide flowers. The 4 petals are in the form of a round-lobed cross tightly surrounding the light-colored stamens and pistil in the center. Douglas's wallflower's fruit resembles an extremely narrow, 4-sided, 2–4-inch-long bean-pod containing a single column of light brown, 1/16–inch seeds.

CULTURE

Although there is considerable taxonomic confusion about this highly variable wildflower, it is easy and rewarding to grow in dry meadows, rock gardens, or conventional beds and borders. Although it is a biennial, Douglas's wallflower will usually produce flowers the first year. It is an excellent choice for sunny borders where long-flowering plants are desired. Not choosy about soils as long as they are well drained, it can tolerate dry conditions once it becomes established. If given enough water in its native range, Douglas's wallflower can sometimes be grown as a perennial.

PROPAGATION

Propagate this plant by seed. Douglas's wallflower is easy to grow — no stratification treatment is needed and seeds will germinate readily. Plant seeds ¼ inch deep, and thin seedlings to 6–8 inches apart. Provide moisture in the spring, when the seedlings are growing most rapidly. In hardiness zones 9 and 10, plant the seeds in the late summer or early fall, and in colder regions start them in pots or flats indoors in the winter and transplant them when danger of frost has passed. Blooming begins in the late spring and continues through the summer.

COMPANIONS

California poppy, purple annual lupine, purple heliotrope, blue dicks, sky lupine, and many others.

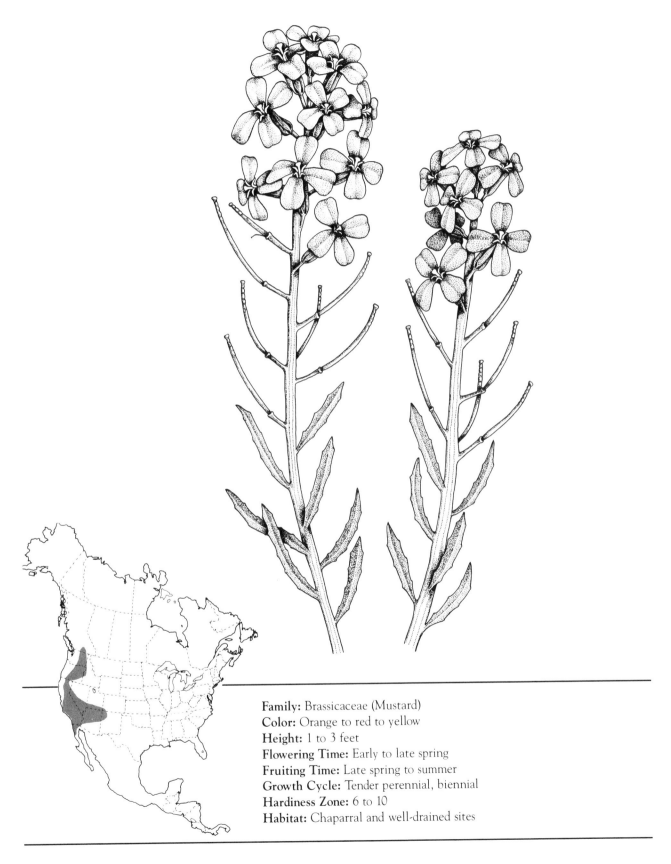

Family: Brassicaceae (Mustard)
Color: Orange to red to yellow
Height: 1 to 3 feet
Flowering Time: Early to late spring
Fruiting Time: Late spring to summer
Growth Cycle: Tender perennial, biennial
Hardiness Zone: 6 to 10
Habitat: Chaparral and well-drained sites

DOUGLAS'S WALLFLOWER (*Erysimum capitatum*)

SHOWY PENSTEMON

Penstemon spectabilis

(Royal penstemon)

Showy penstemon is a relatively tall plant (2–4 feet high) with a spectacular display of up to 100 flowers on the upper half of its stem. The inflated, tubular, 1–1½-inch-long flowers may range in color from blue to violet to rose to pink. The 2 rounded lobes of the upper lip of the flower and the 3 lobes of the lower lip are usually blue, while the inside of the flower is white. The ½-inch-long capsular fruits contain many tiny angular seeds. Showy penstemon has interesting foliage as well, with pairs of bright green, coarsely toothed, 1–4-inch-long leaves clasping the stem. The upper leaves frequently have their bases fused together so that it appears that the stem is growing through them.

CULTURE

Showy penstemons need sunny locations with dry or very well-drained soils. They will tolerate light shade but not wet soils. Do not overwater showy penstemon since they are susceptible to root rot, especially when the plants are dormant. The ideal soil acidity conditions are around neutral (pH 6–8). This is a good plant for dry, infertile soils in sunny locations such as banks and wild gardens.

PROPAGATION

Showy penstemon can be propagated by stem cuttings and root divisions, but propagation by seed is the best method. Plant the seeds in the spring as soon as the soils are warm. The seeds do not require chilling, but may germinate better when exposed to light. Barely scratch them into the surface of the soil and keep moist until the seedlings become established. Alternatively, start them indoors in the late fall or early spring with germination occurring in 2 to 3 weeks. When plants are about 2 months old, transplant them to larger pots or outdoors if danger of frost is past. They will bloom during the first year, so they can be grown as an annual outside their native range. Root divisions in the late fall are another means of propagating this species. Divide rootstock, ensuring that each division has at least one shoot bud, and plant the segments with the bud just at the soil surface. You can also make softwood cuttings from non-flowering shoots during the summer. Plant 6–7-inch cuttings 3 inches deep in sharp sand and keep moist, but not wet, until roots develop. Plant the dormant rootstock in the late fall with the newly formed buds just at the ground surface. This short-lived perennial may need to be replanted every few years, although it often self-seeds.

COMPANIONS

California poppy, prickly poppy, desert marigold, golden yarrow, California bluebell.

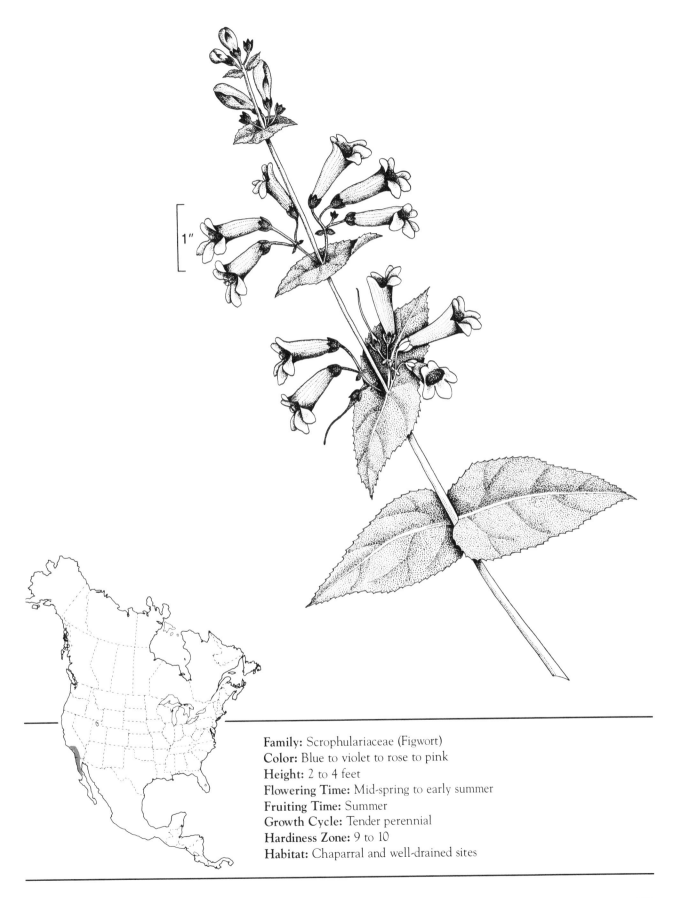

Family: Scrophulariaceae (Figwort)
Color: Blue to violet to rose to pink
Height: 2 to 4 feet
Flowering Time: Mid-spring to early summer
Fruiting Time: Summer
Growth Cycle: Tender perennial
Hardiness Zone: 9 to 10
Habitat: Chaparral and well-drained sites

SHOWY PENSTEMON *(Penstemon spectabilis)*

OUR LORD'S CANDLE

Yucca whipplei

(Spanish bayonet, Quixote plant, chaparral yucca, *quiote*)

Two of the most common names for this plant, "Our Lord's candle" and "Spanish bayonet," seem at odds with each other. The first, given by early Padres in California, refers to the spectacular candelabra of fragrant white flowers. The other, which could have been given by anyone backing into the plant, refers to the unforgiving, spine-tipped, swordlike leaves. The tough, stiff, gray-green leaves of mature plants are 1–3 feet long, rough edged, and arranged like a hemispherical pincushion. The leaves increase in size with age, taking many years to produce the magnificent flowers. Then, a 4–20-foot-tall scape erupts and bears thousands of nodding, creamy white flowers in a 2–4-foot-long cluster. Sometimes the flowers are tinged with lavender or green. Each flower opens in the evening and lasts for several days, but the flowering period takes 2 to 7 weeks to progress from the bottom to the top of the inflorescence. Each of the bell-like, 1–1½-inch flowers has 3 petallike sepals and 3 identical petals. In the center of the flower are 6 stamens with white filaments and golden anthers, and a 3-angled style with a light green, stalked stigma. The fruits of the plant, 1–2-inch-long 6-segmented pods, open when mature and scatter numerous flat, black seeds. Several months after fruiting, the entire plant usually dies, although subspecies from the northern part of the range usually produce new shoots at the base of the dead clump of leaves.

CULTURE

This perennial of the chaparral grows in dry, stony, well-drained soils in open, sunny locations, and may reach 6 feet in diameter. Its natural environment features wet winters and dry summers, so allow the plant to dry out over the summer. It is not hardy and is sensitive to prolonged temperatures below freezing, so it is difficult to maintain this species to the flowering stage in hardiness zones colder than 10. However, it can be grown successfully in cold climates as a pot or container plant the way agaves generally are. If grown in a medium-sized pot, it will grow slowly and remain a manageable, but non-flowering, size for many years.

PROPAGATION

Propagate Our Lord's candle by seed, which require no chilling treatment. Plant in the fall, ¼–½ inch deep in the desired location. Germination may be enhanced by soaking the seeds in water for 2 days before planting them. Thin the seedlings to 2–5 feet apart. Seeds can also be planted in flats and the seedlings carefully transplanted 2–5 feet apart at the end of the first summer. Outside its native range Our Lord's candle will not produce seeds from the flowers because the pollinators are absent (see page 6). You can either attempt to pollinate the flowers by hand or simply buy more seeds from a commercial source. Since the plants die after fruiting, be sure to plant the seeds several years in succession.

COMPANIONS

Golden yarrow, California fuchsia, blazing star, desert mallow, purple heliotrope, desert marigold.

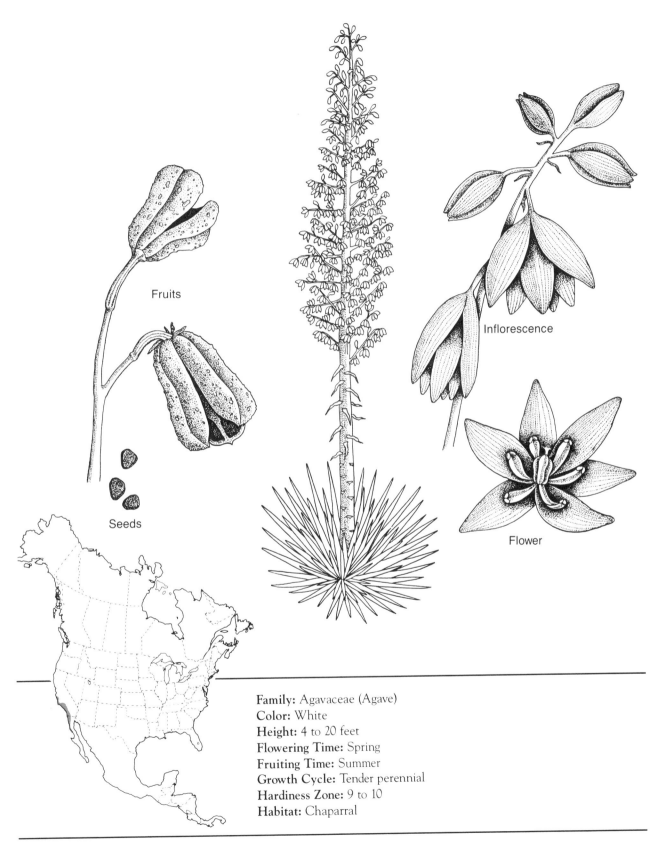

Fruits

Seeds

Inflorescence

Flower

Family: Agavaceae (Agave)
Color: White
Height: 4 to 20 feet
Flowering Time: Spring
Fruiting Time: Summer
Growth Cycle: Tender perennial
Hardiness Zone: 9 to 10
Habitat: Chaparral

OUR LORD'S CANDLE (*Yucca whipplei*)

CALIFORNIA FUCHSIA

Zauschneria californica
(*Epilobium canum*)

(Hummingbird's trumpet, hummingbird flower, *balsamea*)

The Bohemian botanist Theodor Haenke didn't find the Northwest Passage he was searching for in 1791, but he did find this spectacular hummingbird plant and promptly named it in honor of Johann Zauschner, a professor of natural history at the University of Prague. California fuchsia is one of the few plants to flower during the late-summer-to-fall hot season in the Southwest, and its soft green foliage and pendant, vermilion flowers contrast pleasingly with the tan-hued landscape. This often rangy perennial can spread rapidly underground by root sprouts and rhizomes and is more noted for scrambling over the ground than for reaching great heights. It usually grows to less than a foot high and when not flowering appears to be a rather disorganized tangle of narrow, ½–1½-inch-long, soft, lightly woolly leaves attached to the branching stems that emerge from its extensive root system. The stems become woody near their bases, while loose clusters of bright red flowers are borne at their tips. The 1–1½-inch-long flowers have 4 petals and 4 petallike sepals that fuse together forming a tube. The 8 stamens and 4-lobed stigma, projecting beyond the throat of the flower, remind one of a fuchsia, another member of the evening primrose family. The dark red inferior ovary elongates after hummingbirds have pollinated the flowers, and the withering corolla is shed as the 4-chambered, capsular fruit develops. When ripe, the fruit splits open and releases its cargo of 1/16-inch, oblong, tufted seeds onto the breezes.

CULTURE Grow California fuchsia in full sun on well-drained soils. It grows best on dry sandy or stony soils with a pH of 7.0–8.0, and should not be given additional water in the summer if planted on heavy, clay soil that remains wet for a long time. It is remarkably drought tolerant and ideal as a ground cover on hot, dry, sunny slopes, banks, and hillsides where it can spread without intruding on other plantings. It can also be used effectively as edging and in rock gardens. If it becomes too unkempt-looking, pinch back the young shoots to give the plants a bushier form. In coastal regions California fuchsia remains evergreen throughout the year, but in areas colder than hardiness zone 9 it dies back to the root crown each winter. In coastal northern California it can flower from late summer into the winter.

PROPAGATION California fuchsia is very easily propagated by seed, root division, or stem cuttings. Sow untreated seeds in the desired locations in the early spring. Thin the seedlings to about 2 feet apart to allow for spreading. Make stem cuttings in the fall, keep moist but not wet until established, and in regions colder than hardiness zone 9 give some winter protection the first year. The roots of large established plants can be divided in the early spring and replanted 2–3 feet apart.

COMPANIONS Usually California fuchsia is grown by itself, although it makes an interesting underplanting for Our Lord's candle.

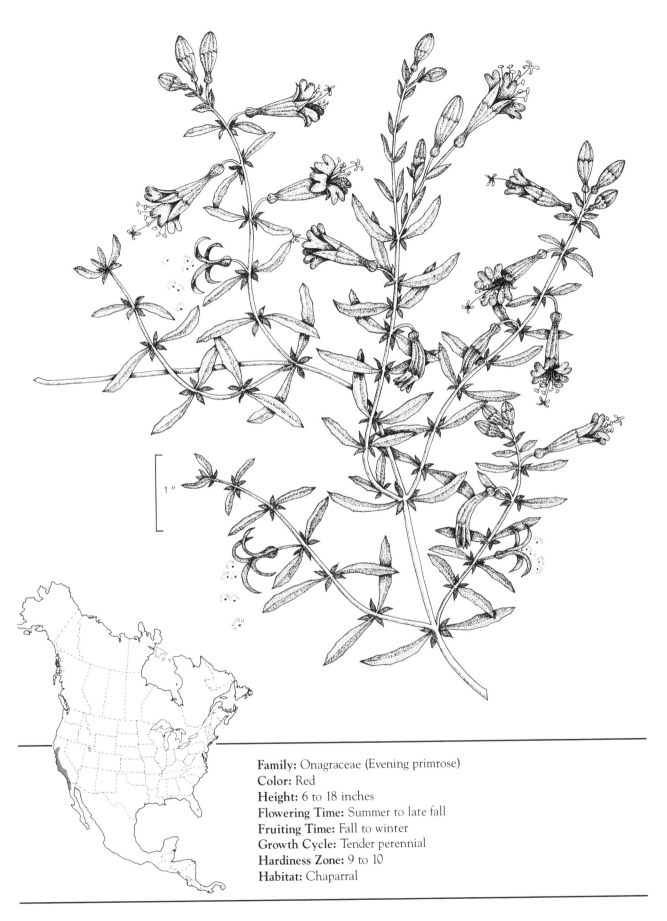

1"

Family: Onagraceae (Evening primrose)
Color: Red
Height: 6 to 18 inches
Flowering Time: Summer to late fall
Fruiting Time: Fall to winter
Growth Cycle: Tender perennial
Hardiness Zone: 9 to 10
Habitat: Chaparral

CALIFORNIA FUCHSIA (*Zauschneria californica*)

FOOTHILL SPECIES

This section presents species that grow in the varied environments of the foothills bordering grasslands, deserts, and coastal areas. Foothills typically have more moisture available and the species in this section tend to respond to additional water in the late spring. These species also tolerate partial shade, since they flourish among the scattered trees that grow in the foothills. Most of these species, however, can also be grown in full sunlight under normal garden conditions.

Oaks make a natural complement to native grasses in the foothill landscape. The evergreen **coast live oak** (*Quercus agrifolia*) with its elongated acorns should be considered if you live near the Pacific Ocean, while the **valley oak** (*Quercus lobata*) and **California buckeye** (*Aesculus californica*) both lose their leaves in the summer and are ideal for inland situations. Valley oak has attractive round-lobed, deep green leaves and grows to 70 feet or more. California buckeye is more shrubby, typically reaching 20 feet, and produces plumes of creamy pink flowers in late spring and early summer.

Wildflowers can be interplanted with shrubs and trees to create a more natural foothill woodland landscape. In addition to the species presented here and in the sections on grassland and chaparral species, **chia** (*Salvia columbariae*) and **hummingbird** or **pitcher sage** (*Salvia spathacea*) make excellent additions to foothill gardens. Chia is a small annual sage with flowers that emerge in the spring from a whorled rosette of gray-green, fernlike leaves. The 1 to 4 round clusters of bright blue flowers, surrounded by magenta bracts, sit atop a 1–2-foot-high stem. Chia produces edible seeds that were a staple for Native Americans in California and Mexico. Hummingbird sage is a taller, perennial wildflower, reaching 3 feet under ideal conditions. It has pairs of rough, light green, lance-shaped leaves scattered along its stem, topped by cylindrical clusters of crimson flowers with purple bracts. As its name suggests, this species attracts hummingbirds. It makes an ideal plant for wooded areas, for while it thrives on moisture, it can tolerate drought and even fire. It may become a bit weedy over time, but is a beautiful weed at that.

Red ribbons (*Clarkia concinna*) is an annual wildflower associated with oak woodlands. Its intriguing bright rose petals are deeply lobed and look some-

Foothill woodland garden

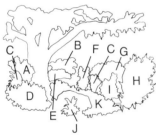

A. Blazing star
B. Lomatium
C. Purple needlegrass
D. Sky lupine
E. Linanthus
F. Chinese houses
G. Indian pink
H. Giant evening primrose
I. Coralbells
J. Pine bluegrass
K. Baby blue-eyes

what shredded. An excellent companion to **Chinese houses**, it likewise grows best in moist, shady sites. Ravines and depressions in foothill woodlands may have sufficient moisture to grow ferns, and **giant chain fern** (*Woodwardia fimbriata*) is one of the easiest to grow. Its clumps of 2–6-foot high evergreen fronds make an excellent background planting.

Numerous large shrubs and small trees are superb additions to the foothill garden. **Western redbud** (*Cercis occidentalis*), a small drought-resistant tree, grows to 15 feet and has beautiful clusters of pink-magenta, pealike flowers that appear in the late winter and early spring just before the heart-shaped, lustrous leaves. The leaves turn a striking bronze-red in the autumn just before they fall. If your garden is above 2,000 feet in elevation and sufficiently large, **western dogwood** (*Cornus nuttallii*) is a spectacular small tree to be considered. This 30–60-foot-high tree has many clusters of small green flowers surrounded by 4 large, creamy, petallike bracts filling the late spring foothills with splashes of white. By autumn, both the fruits and oval leaves turn from green to red and orange. Be sure to plant western dogwood in well-drained sites and avoid excess watering during the spring and summer. The elliptical, leathery evergreen leaves of **madrone** (*Arbutus menziesii*) contrast exquisitely with its beautiful red bark. In the spring this 40-foot tree produces clusters of white urn-shaped flowers that, by autumn, mature into bright red-orange fruits, attracting many species of birds. It may take 10 years or so for small trees to grow sufficiently to produce flowers, but it is worth the wait.

CHINESE HOUSES

Collinsia heterophylla
(C. bicolor)

(Innocence, collinsia)

The common name Chinese houses refers to the whorled pagoda effect of tiers of lavender-blue and white flowers encircling the top of this plant's stem. Each of the individual ¾-inch-long flowers has a 2-lobed upper lip of pale blue to white and a 3-lobed violet to purple lower lip. All the upper lobes have maroon dots at their bases. The middle lobe of the lower lip is folded into a pouch containing the 4 stamens, the long style, and the nectar-producing glands. Insects usually transfer pollen between anthers and stigmas on different plants, but Chinese houses can produce seeds even if pollen is transferred between flowers on the same plant. The ¼-inch round capsular fruits contain many brown, ovoid, 1/16-inch seeds. The bright green, 1–2-inch-long, lance-shaped leaves have toothed edges and clasp the 1–2-foot-high stem. A velvety fuzz often covers the entire plant, including the flowers. Chinese houses were discovered by the Scottish botanist David Douglas, who recognized their horticultural value and introduced them into European gardens.

CULTURE   Chinese houses grow best in light shade and moist, well-drained, rich soils, although they will tolerate light conditions from full sun to shade. Be sure to provide moderate moisture and shade from the heat of the day if growing this plant in zones 9 or 10. Elsewhere this plant will do quite well under normal garden soil, moisture, and light conditions. In fact, this species used to be a popular garden plant in the eastern U.S. and was called "innocence" even though it frequently escaped the garden and became naturalized far beyond its natural range. A hardy annual, it is ideal for rock gardens, shaded borders, plantings at the bases of trees, ground cover for bulbs, and cut flowers. The flowering season can be prolonged by removing the withering flowers before the fruit has set, or by staggering the planting dates.

PROPAGATION   Sow seeds in both the fall and early spring for the maximum season of flowering, but be sure to provide extra moisture in the late spring, especially if it is a dry year. Plant the seeds 1/8–1/4 inch deep in the desired location and keep moist, but not wet, until flowering is completed. Chinese houses will self-seed once established.

COMPANIONS   Baby blue-eyes, coralbells, farewell-to-spring, linanthus, purple annual lupine, western shooting star.

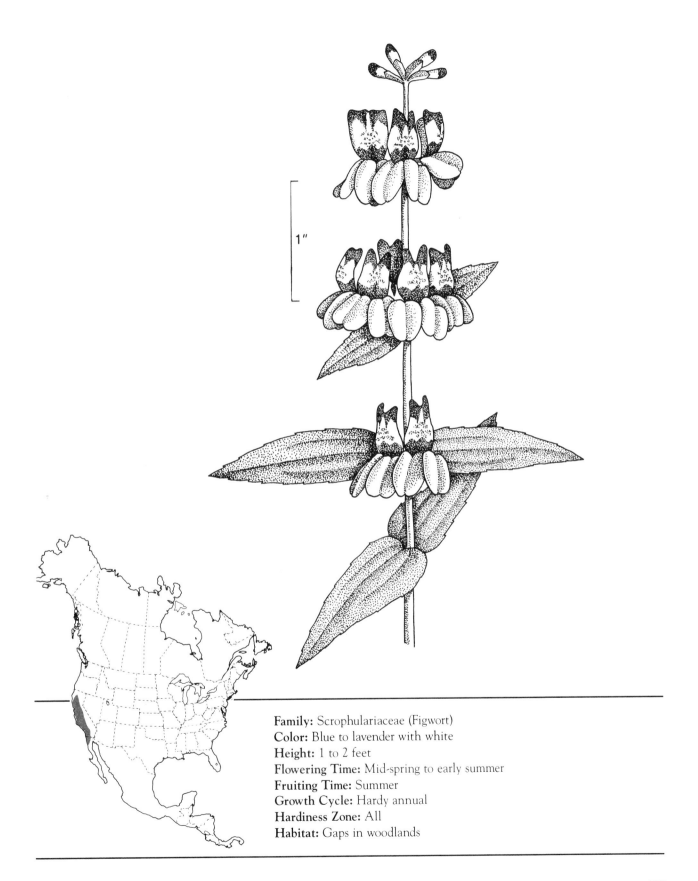

Family: Scrophulariaceae (Figwort)
Color: Blue to lavender with white
Height: 1 to 2 feet
Flowering Time: Mid-spring to early summer
Fruiting Time: Summer
Growth Cycle: Hardy annual
Hardiness Zone: All
Habitat: Gaps in woodlands

1"

CHINESE HOUSES (*Collinsia heterophylla*) 137

CORALBELLS

Heuchera sanguinea

This lovely, hardy perennial, a favorite in European and North American gardens, is a native of moist, shady areas in the mountains of the Southwest. Coralbells, like other members of the saxifrage family, has a mound of heart-shaped, geranium-like leaves. In the long days between April and August a velvety, 1–2-foot scape rises from the mound of leaves, bearing loose clusters of pink to bright red, bell-like flowers. Each of the ¼–½-inch-long flowers has 5 red sepals and 5 small, lobed, red petals. While bees are the main pollinator of coralbells, hummingbirds also find this wildflower attractive.

CULTURE

In hot, arid locations coralbells should be planted in shade to partial shade. It grows best in soils that are slightly acid (pH 6–7), although it is not terribly choosy as long as the soil is moist throughout the summer. The long scape, low foliage, and long-lasting flowers make coralbells an excellent plant for shady borders, rock gardens, cut flowers, and at the edges of beds of taller plants.

PROPAGATION

Coralbells are easily propagated by seed, division, or leaf cuttings. Light stimulates seed germination, so plant the seeds only 1/8 inch deep at most. Plant fresh, ripe seeds in flats in the summer, or plant commercially available seeds in the spring or fall. Germination takes 2 to 3 weeks in the spring once temperatures reach 70°F, and the plants will flower the second year. To propagate vegetatively, divide roots in the late fall or early spring, ensuring that each division has several buds. Plant the divisions 10–15 inches apart with the buds just at the soil surface. If leaves are cut in the late summer or fall, set in moist sand, and given light shade, they will root easily and can be transplanted when roots are fully developed. After 3 or 4 years coralbells will enlarge into massive clumps that should be divided in the spring, discarding the old woody material, to encourage new growth and more abundant flowering.

COMPANIONS

Chinese houses, blazing star, western shooting star, Douglas's iris, blue-eyed grass, checker bloom.

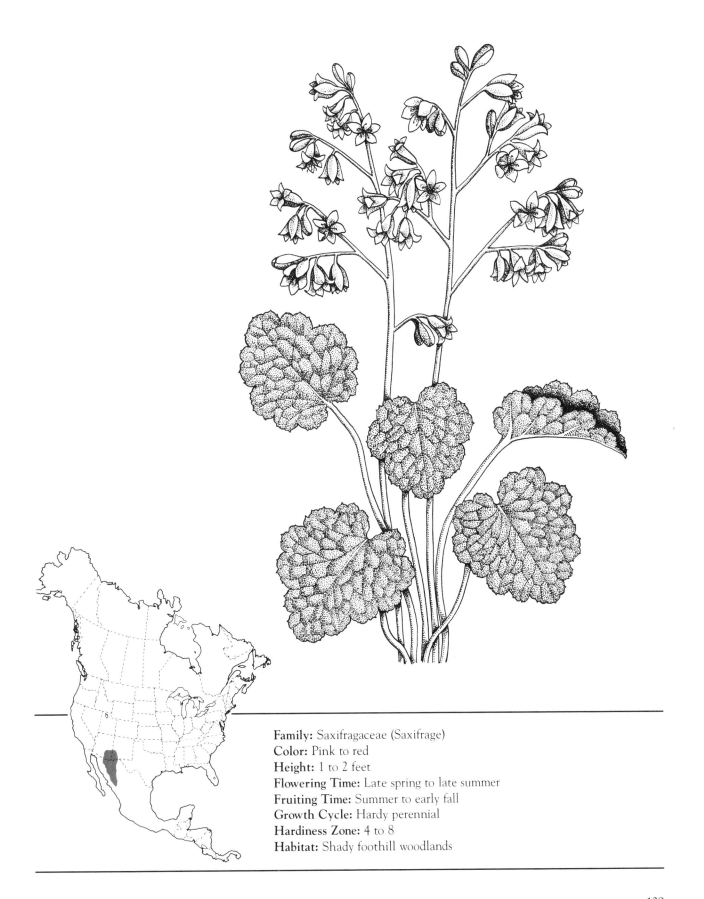

Family: Saxifragaceae (Saxifrage)
Color: Pink to red
Height: 1 to 2 feet
Flowering Time: Late spring to late summer
Fruiting Time: Summer to early fall
Growth Cycle: Hardy perennial
Hardiness Zone: 4 to 8
Habitat: Shady foothill woodlands

CORALBELLS *(Heuchera sanguinea)*

LINANTHUS

Linanthus grandiflorus

(Mountain phlox, California phlox, large-flowered linanthus)

Linanthus is a strikingly beautiful spring annual of the Coastal Ranges in California. The 4–20-inch-high stems are encircled by whorls of dark green leaves, deeply cleft into inch-long, linear, tinelike segments. Dense clusters of silky white, inch-long, trumpet-shaped flowers tinged with pink or lavender are borne at the tops of the stems. The hairy calyx surrounds the flower tube, which opens into 5 broad petals. Inside the throat of the flower tube 5 golden stamens are visible above the stigmas and the ring of tufted hairs. Linanthus has a capsular fruit with irregularly angled, light brown, membrane-coated, 1/16-inch seeds.

CULTURE

In its native Coastal Range habitat, linanthus forms dense colonies in the spring and then usually dies out during the summer dry season, but its long flowering period can be prolonged by periodic watering. Plant this annual in the full sun on light, sandy soils. The soil should be moist, but not wet, while the seedlings are growing rapidly in the spring, and then irrigated only if it becomes overly dry.

PROPAGATION

Sow the seeds 1/8–1/4 inch deep in their desired locations. The seeds require no chilling treatment and should be planted in the fall in hardiness zones 9 and 10 for flowering in April and May. Elsewhere plant them in the spring after the soil warms up.

COMPANIONS

Coralbells, sky lupine, California poppy, wind poppy, tidy tips, baby blue-eyes, other West Coast annuals.

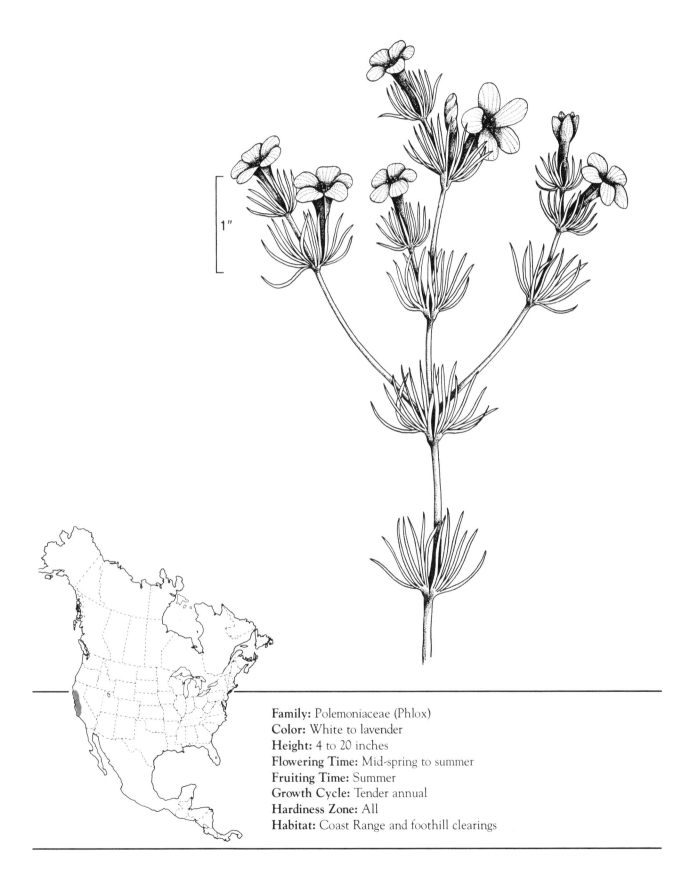

Family: Polemoniaceae (Phlox)
Color: White to lavender
Height: 4 to 20 inches
Flowering Time: Mid-spring to summer
Fruiting Time: Summer
Growth Cycle: Tender annual
Hardiness Zone: All
Habitat: Coast Range and foothill clearings

LINANTHUS *(Linanthus grandiflorus)*

LOMATIUM

Lomatium's lacy foliage and clusters of fuzzy white flowers cascade down dry ridges and slopes in spring in coastal California. Shoots of this low-growing perennial emerge during the winter from a long, thick, extensively branched tap root. Each lomatium plant has up to 10 short, flattened stems that grow for several inches along the ground, then rise and turn purplish just as the clusters of flowers appear in early spring. The 3–8-inch-long main leaves, whose bases clasp and nearly encircle the stem, are divided 4 times into small, delicate leaflets. Ten to twenty pompom clusters of tiny, 5-petaled, greenish yellow flowers arise on 2-inch-long stalks from the bases of the lower leaves. The flowers appear creamy white because of the abundant fuzzy hairs that cover the petals and flower stalks. The woolly fruits are rather showy, up to ¾ inch long and ½ inch broad, and have broad, membranous, reddish wings that catch the wind and aid in dispersing the seeds considerable distances. The shape of the fruit inspired its Latin name: *Lomatium* comes from the Greek word loma or "border," referring to the broad wings, while *dasycarpum* translates to "thick fruit." The entire top of the plant dies back to the root crown during the summer dry season.

CULTURE

Grow lomatium in full sun to partial shade on well-drained soils. While this plant can tolerate dry summer conditions, the number of plants in a colony in any given year depends on the amount of moisture during the growing season. If the winter is dry and cold, growth of the plant is less vigorous and flowering is reduced. Lomatium is an excellent plant for rock gardens and sunny banks even though it can become weedy and has active growth only from winter through spring. The dead leaves can be pulled off during the summer.

PROPAGATION

Although lomatium is a perennial, it is easiest to propagate from seeds, which require no treatment. Plant seeds ¼–½ inches deep in the desired locations during the fall. Keep moist until germination starts and provide the developing seedlings with moisture until the winter rains settle in. Plants from seeds usually flower the second spring.

COMPANIONS

Checker bloom, showy penstemon, golden yarrow, blazing star.

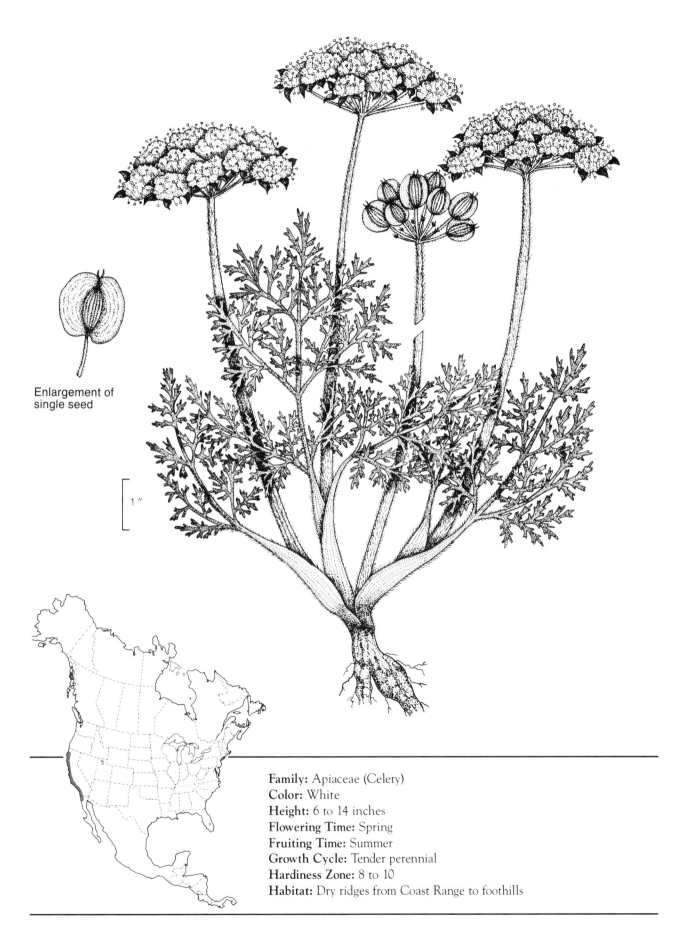

Enlargement of
single seed

1 ″

Family: Apiaceae (Celery)
Color: White
Height: 6 to 14 inches
Flowering Time: Spring
Fruiting Time: Summer
Growth Cycle: Tender perennial
Hardiness Zone: 8 to 10
Habitat: Dry ridges from Coast Range to foothills

LOMATIUM *(Lomatium dasycarpum)*

SKY LUPINE

Lupinus nanus

(Field lupine, Douglas's lupine, *lupino, altramuz*)

The flowers of this petite annual lupine mirror the coastal California skies in springtime, with whorls of blue and white pealike flowers atop 4–20-inch stems. Each of the ½-inch-long flowers has a rich blue top petal, known as a banner. At its base is a white or yellow spot flecked with dark blue. The lateral petals, or wings, and the 2 lower petals fused into the "keel" are clear blue. A short fuzzy beanlike pod contains 4 to 8 gray-brown, mottled, ⅛-inch seeds, which are ejected as the fruits ripen. The leaves of sky lupine are palmately compound with 5 to 7 narrow, inch-long leaflets covered with long hairs.

CULTURE
Grow this annual in full sun on soils that are on the dry side, like sandy loams and dryish clayey loams. The seedlings need moisture in the early spring while they become established, but little water is needed once flowering starts. Overwatering can lead to mildew problems. If inoculation is necessary to establish sky lupine in your soil, use Lupinus rhizobia (Nitragin-type Lupinus special #2). Snails seem to relish the young seedlings and may need to be controlled if they are abundant. Sky lupine is an ideal plant for massing on dry, barren banks.

PROPAGATION
As with other annuals, sky lupine is propagated only by seed. To collect the seeds in the wild, gather the pods when they turn brown and place them in a paper bag. Fold the top of the bag closed so the seeds aren't shot out while you have your back turned. The seeds do not require chilling treatment, but do require scarification in order to germinate. Rub the seeds briskly between two sheets of medium-grit sandpaper to scratch the seed coat and allow moisture to enter. Soaking the seeds in warm (180°F) water and then cooling them in the water overnight will also enhance germination. Plant the seeds in the late fall or winter, ¼ inch deep, in the desired location since it is difficult to transplant seedlings. Germination takes 2 to 3 weeks at 68°F, and seedlings should be thinned to 2–3 inches apart after a month or so. In their native range sky lupines generally self-seed.

COMPANIONS
California poppy, tidy tips, Douglas's wallflower, golden yarrow, goldfields, farewell-to-spring, Indian pink.

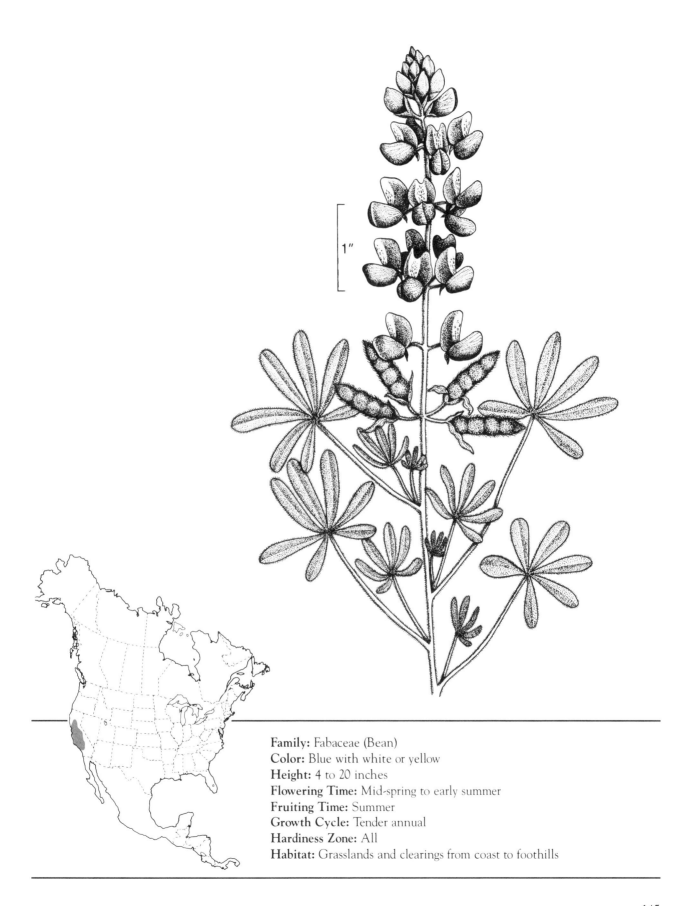

Family: Fabaceae (Bean)
Color: Blue with white or yellow
Height: 4 to 20 inches
Flowering Time: Mid-spring to early summer
Fruiting Time: Summer
Growth Cycle: Tender annual
Hardiness Zone: All
Habitat: Grasslands and clearings from coast to foothills

SKY LUPINE (*Lupinus nanus*)

BLAZING STAR

(Evening star)

Not only does this 5-petaled star come out in the evening, but it also has a meteor shower of golden stamens at its center. This 1–4-foot-high annual has 2–3-inch-long, clasping, coarsely toothed, hairy, dandelion-like leaves scattered along its hairy stems. Groups of 2 to 3 fragrant, 2–3-inch, golden yellow flowers open in the evening at the tops of the plant and usually close by noon of the next day. The individual flowers have 5 broad, rounded petals with pointed tips, frequently with splotches of red-orange at their bases. Many long stamens with yellow anthers lie flat against the petals as the flower opens, but rise in a cluster at the center of the flower by the following morning. The 1–1½-inch-long, hairy, capsular fruit is filled with many small (1/16-inch), angular seeds. Blazing star is yet another stunning California native plant discovered by David Douglas and sent back to his native Britain to be introduced into gardens there.

CULTURE Blazing star should be grown on moist to dry soils in the full sun. Well-drained soils are essential for successfully maintaining this plant, which is otherwise adaptable to sandy or loamy soils of just about any fertility. Soil should be kept moist until flowering starts and then should be allowed to dry out. Blazing star will tolerate heat, wind, and poor soils as long as the drainage is good, as in heavy, clay soils the plants are prone to root rots. It is most attractive when planted in large gardens or naturalized in meadows, rather than confined to small spaces.

PROPAGATION This annual is propagated by seed, which should be sown in the late fall or early winter in hardiness zones 9 and 10, and in the early spring elsewhere. The seed does not require chilling treatment and will germinate in about 2 to 3 weeks. Plant the seeds 1/8 inch deep in well-drained soil where desired and thin seedlings to 6 inches apart. Blazing star generally starts to flower in April and once established will freely self-seed.

COMPANIONS California poppy, sky lupine, purple annual lupine, showy penstemon, purple heliotrope.

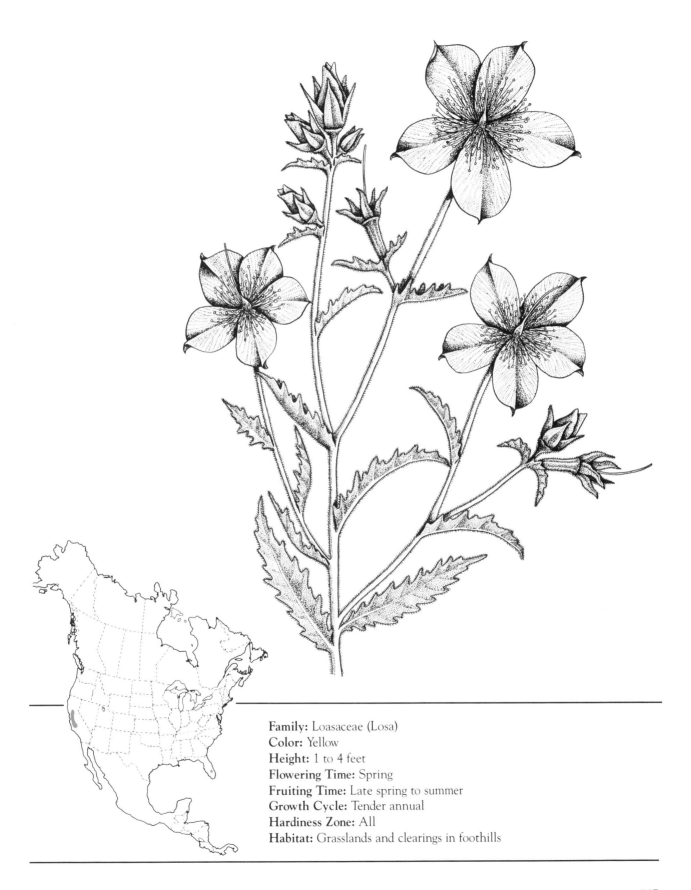

Family: Loasaceae (Losa)
Color: Yellow
Height: 1 to 4 feet
Flowering Time: Spring
Fruiting Time: Late spring to summer
Growth Cycle: Tender annual
Hardiness Zone: All
Habitat: Grasslands and clearings in foothills

BLAZING STAR *(Mentzelia lindleyi)*

BABY BLUE-EYES

Nemophila menziesii

(California bluebells, *Mariana*, *azuleja*)

Some botanists divide baby blue-eyes into 3 three separate species based on their form and flower color. As Europeans have known for over a century, however, any of the forms are easily grown and make attractive additions to the garden. On the spreading, straggling, branched stems are pairs of 1–2-inch-long, somewhat hairy leaves resembling those of the dandelion, except that they are round-lobed instead of pointed. Atop the 10–20-inch stems are 1–1½-inch-wide flowers with 5 broad petals, 5 stamens with dark anthers, and a pistil with a branched style. Most often the petals are blue at the rounded tip and white with blue flecks or radiating streaks at the base, but in some forms the petals are all blue, or sky blue with dark blue dots at their bases. The color of this wildflower inspired its Spanish common names — *Mariana* or "Mary's flower" refers to the color of the Virgin Mary's robe, and *azuleja* means "little blue one." Bees visit the flowers in search of nectar and remove the pollen several days before the stigma becomes fully exposed, a pattern that enhances cross pollination, although individual flowers are self-fertile. Baby blue-eyes' flowers open and close in response to air temperature, the petals folding inward at night or in the cold. Extremely hot weather, however, shortens its flowering season. The fruit is a round, hairy, ¼–½-inch capsule containing 10 to 20 dark, 1/8-inch seeds. Baby blue-eyes has been a popular garden plant in Great Britain since it was introduced by the London Horticultural Society in 1833.

CULTURE
The Latin name *Nemophila* means "lover of the grove" and this hardy annual grows best in partial shade to full sun, on well-drained soils that are moist but not wet. The flowering season is relatively short but can be prolonged if the soil is kept moist while the plants are in flower. Baby blue-eyes is adaptable to the usual range of soil nutrient and pH conditions found in most gardens, and is easy to cultivate. It makes an excellent cover for beds of bulbs.

PROPAGATION
In hardiness zones 9 and 10 plant seeds in the fall, and elsewhere plant in the early spring. In fall seeds germinate quickly and the seedling will remain as a rosette of leaves until flowering the next spring. The seeds, which require no chilling treatment for germination, should be planted 1/8 inch deep in desired locations. Germination is most rapid (1 to 2 weeks) when the seeds are kept moist and are planted when the day length is relatively short and the soil temperature is below 70°F. Baby blue-eyes usually self-seed.

COMPANIONS
California poppy, tidy tips, Chinese houses, western shooting star, linanthus, farewell-to-spring.

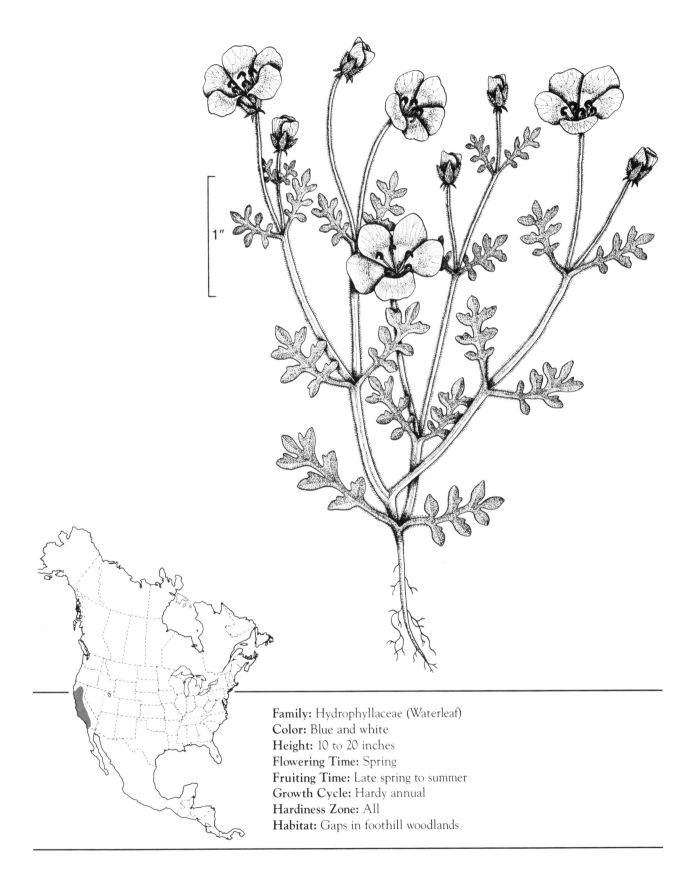

Family: Hydrophyllaceae (Waterleaf)
Color: Blue and white
Height: 10 to 20 inches
Flowering Time: Spring
Fruiting Time: Late spring to summer
Growth Cycle: Hardy annual
Hardiness Zone: All
Habitat: Gaps in foothill woodlands

BABY BLUE-EYES (*Nemophila menziesii*)

GIANT EVENING PRIMROSE

Oenothera hookeri
(*O. elata* subsp. *hookeri*)

(Hooker's evening primrose, *coscatlacualtzin*, *hierba de Santiago*)

This is one of the largest and showiest of the evening primroses. There are several naturally occurring subspecies of this taxonomically diverse plant with differing heights and varying flower sizes. The giant evening primrose is usually 3–5 feet tall, although there are reports of plants ranging from 1–9 feet in height. Regardless of the eventual height of the stem, this biennial spends its first year as a low rosette of leaves. The second year the stem bolts and numerous 5–10-inch-long leaves appear scattered along the reddish stem. The leaves, stems, and bases of the flower clusters are frequently covered with soft hairs. Clusters of bright yellow, saucer-shaped flowers are borne at the tops of the stems. To the human eye the petals appear to be a uniform rich yellow, but to the bees that pollinate this species and can see ultraviolet light, the flowers display yellow and purple petals. Each of the 2½–3½-inch flowers has 4 broad petals which one can watch unfurl in late afternoon or at dusk. The evening blossoming of flowers gives this plant its common name, although it is not related to the true primroses. The short-lived flowers wither in the noonday sun, turning orange with age. The fruit is a slender, woody, 1–2-inch-long capsule containing many tiny seeds. Giant evening primrose is named in honor of the British botanist Sir William Jackson Hooker, a 19th-century director of the Royal Botanic Garden at Kew.

CULTURE

Giant evening primrose should be planted in full sun and given ample room since it tends to become weedy. It is not fussy about soil acidity conditions, and while it grows best in moist soils, it is tolerant of moderately dry soils as well. This biennial, an excellent plant for large damp meadows and streamside plantings, can be grown in hardiness zones 4 to 10.

PROPAGATION

The easiest way to propagate giant evening primrose is from seed. Seed planted in the fall should be scratched into the surface of the soil where the plants are desired, and kept moist. No stratification of the seed is needed. Thin the seedlings to 12–18 inches apart or more. Seedlings will form a rosette the first season and flower the second season. As with other biennials, it is a good idea to plant the seeds 2 successive years to establish a continuously flowering population.

COMPANIONS

Golden yarrow, purple heliotrope, blue-eyed grass.

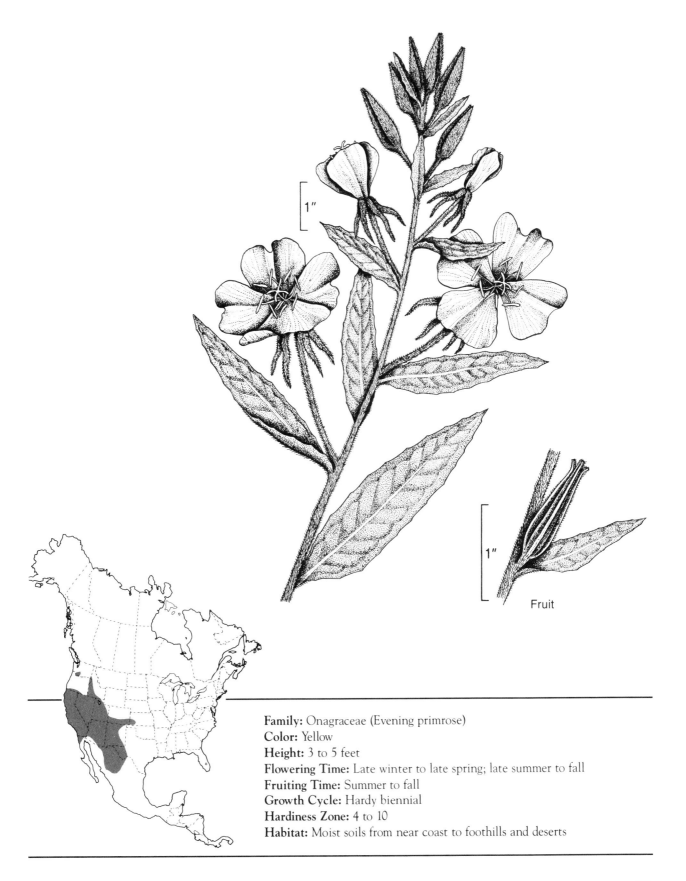

1"

1"

Fruit

Family: Onagraceae (Evening primrose)
Color: Yellow
Height: 3 to 5 feet
Flowering Time: Late winter to late spring; late summer to fall
Fruiting Time: Summer to fall
Growth Cycle: Hardy biennial
Hardiness Zone: 4 to 10
Habitat: Moist soils from near coast to foothills and deserts

GIANT EVENING PRIMROSE (*Oenothera hookeri*)

INDIAN PINK

Silene californica

This pink is bright red — atop its several 6–18-inch branched stems are showy scarlet flowers 1–1½ inches across. The flowers have 5 broad petals, each with 4 round-tipped lobes, a narrow outer pair and a wide inner pair. The 3 styles and 10 stamens protrude from the center of the flower. A 1-inch tubular calyx with 5 teeth surrounds the base of the flower, and later covers the 1-inch elongated capsular fruit until it ruptures open to reveal numerous red-brown seeds. The pairs of 1½-3-inch-long dark green leaves, like the stems they clasp, are covered with minute, sticky, soft hairs. As the fruits ripen in the summer, the foliage dries out and withers. Indian pink's tap root may be 4 inches long.

CULTURE

Indian pink will grow well in light shade to partial sun. Although it needs moderate moisture during the start of the flowering season, the soil should be dry as the plant enters dormancy in the last half of the summer. While the soil should be well drained, Indian pink is relatively indifferent to soil acidity conditions. This perennial is not hardy enough to be grown in regions colder than hardiness zone 8. But even in other regions it is worth the effort, even if one has to use deep flower pots and move them seasonally to match the plant's environmental preferences.

PROPAGATION

Indian pink should be propagated by seed since it is difficult to divide the deep tap root. In its native range, plant the seeds 1/8 inch deep in the fall in the desired locations. Elsewhere plant Indian pink in the spring where desired or at the surface of deep pots. The seeds do not require stratification treatment, but germination may be slow and erratic. The first year the seedlings will produce few leaves, but an extensive tap root. If pots are used, leave the seedlings in the pot until the fall and then carefully transplant the dormant roots, disturbing them as little as possible, 8-12 inches apart with the root crown just below the soil surface. Grown from seed Indian pink will flower the second year.

COMPANIONS

Blue dicks, Chinese houses, Douglas's wallflower, baby blue-eyes, purple annual lupine, blazing star.

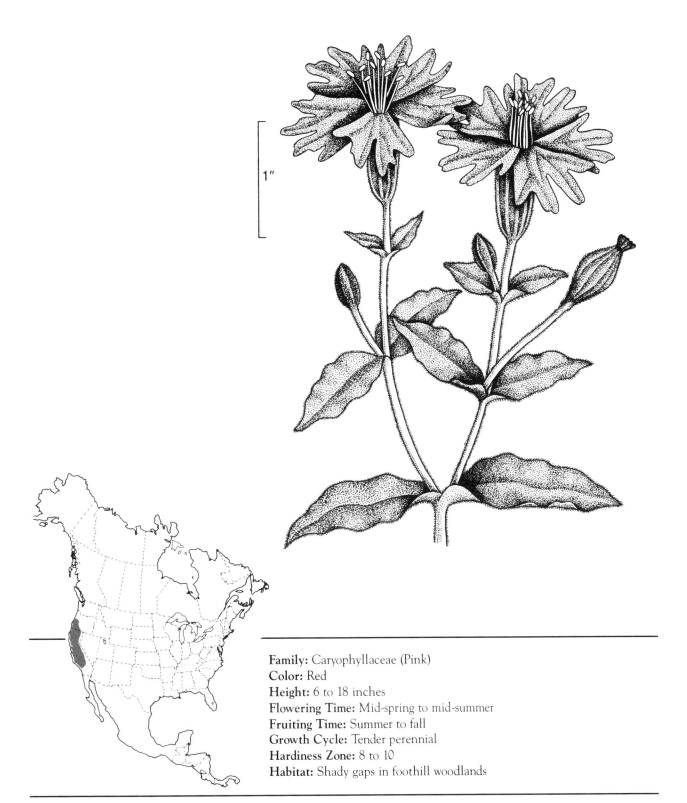

1"

Family: Caryophyllaceae (Pink)
Color: Red
Height: 6 to 18 inches
Flowering Time: Mid-spring to mid-summer
Fruiting Time: Summer to fall
Growth Cycle: Tender perennial
Hardiness Zone: 8 to 10
Habitat: Shady gaps in foothill woodlands

INDIAN PINK *(Silene californica)*

Appendixes

Suppliers

Arizona

Desert Enterprises
P.O. Box 23
Morristown, AZ 85342
(602)388-2448

Sells seeds retail and wholesale, by phone only. Can ship to just about all points in U.S. and Europe. Lists free. Custom mixes of wildflowers, cacti, desert shrubs, native grasses, trees.

Hubbs Brothers Seed Company
1522 N. 35th Street
Phoenix, AZ 85008
(602)267-8132

Sells seeds retail and wholesale, by mail order and phone order. Free catalog. Native seeds from Sonoran & Mojave Deserts.

Mountain States Wholesale Nursery
P.O. Box 33982
Phoenix, AZ 85067
(602)247-8509

Sells live plants wholesale, over the counter and by phone order. Ships all year. Free catalog. Native and drought-tolerant container-grown nursery stock.

Southwestern Native Seeds
Box 50503
Tucson, AZ 85703

Sells seeds retail by mail order. Catalog $1.00. Ornamental flowers and shrubs.

Wild Seed
P.O. Box 27751
Tempe, AZ 85285
(602)968-9751

Sells seeds wholesale by mail order and phone order. Free catalog. Southwestern desert & mountain wildflowers, mixes.

California

Blue Oak Nursery
2731 Mountain Oak Lane
Rescue, CA 95672
(916)677-2111

Sells live plants retail and wholesale, by mail order and phone order. Free catalog. Specializing in western state natives, drought-tolerant plants. Sells over the counter.

C. H. Baccus
900 Boynton Avenue
San Jose, CA 95117

Sells live plants retail by mail order. Ships in September and October. Free catalog. Native bulbs of the Western states, calochortus, fritillaria, brodin.

California Flora Nursery
P.O. Box 3
Somers and D Streets
Fulton, CA 95439
(707)528-8813

Sells live plants retail and wholesale, over the counter and by phone order. Delivers within a 60-mile radius. Plant list available. California natives, Mediterranean and unusual perennials.

Carter Seeds
475 Mar Vista Drive
Vista, CA 92083
(800)872-7711

Sells seeds retail and wholesale, by mail order or phone order. Free catalog.

Common Ground Garden Supply
2225 El Camino Real
Palo Alto, CA 94306
(415)328-6752

Non-profit organization. Sells seeds retail. Wildflower seed mixes for different habitats, and special orders. Tues.—Sat. 10 am—5 pm.

E & H Products
78260 Darby Road
Bermuda Dunes, CA 92201
(619)345-0147

Sells seeds retail and wholesale, by mail order or phone order. Catalog $1.00.

Environmental Seed Producers, Inc.
P.O. Box 5904
El Monte, CA 91734
(818)442-3330

Sells seeds wholesale only. Specializes in California natives.

J. L. Hudson, Seedsman
P.O. Box 1058
Redwood City, CA 94064

Sells seeds retail and wholesale, by mail order. Catalog $1.00. Wildflowers & rare plants from around the world.

Las Palitas Nursery
Star Route Box 23X, Las Palitas Road
Santa Margarita, CA 93453

Sells seeds and plants, retail and whole-sale, by mail order. Ships live plants in spring and fall, throughout U.S. Catalog $4.00. Specializes in annual seeds, live perennials, shrubs, trees native to California.

Moon Mountain West
P.O. Box 34, 864 Nappa Avenue
Morro Bay, CA 93442

Sells wildflower seeds retail and whole-sale, mail order or over the counter. Will ship bulk or by the packet. Catalog $1.00. Specializes in California natives, but produces regional mixtures as well.

Native Sons Wholesale Nursery
379 West El Campo Road
Arrroyo Grande, CA 93420
(805)481-5996

Sells live plants wholesale. Ships year-round to San Francisco and Los Angeles area. Specializes in natives and drought-tolerant plants.

Pacific Nurseries of California, Inc.
2099 Hillside Boulevard
Colma, CA 94014

Sells live plants wholesale. Trees and shrubs. Free catalog.

Pacific Tree Farms
4301 Lynnwood Drive
Chula Vista, CA 92010
(619)422-2400

Sells seeds and live plants, retail and wholesale, by mail order and phone order. Catalog $1.50. Natives for mild climates.

The Theodore Payne Foundation
10459 Tuxford Street
Sun Valley, CA 91352
(818)768-1802

Sells seeds and live plants retail and wholesale, by mail order, over the counter, and phone order. No shipping. Catalogs $1.00. 450 species of seeds; 600 species of plants.

Peaceful Valley Farm Supply
P.O. Box 2209
Grass Valley, CA 95945
(916)272-4769

Sells seeds retail and wholesale, by mail order, over the counter, and phone order. Minimum order of $20.00; U.P.S. avail-able out of California, big orders by truck. Catalog $2.00. Organic growing supplies, flower bulbs, tools, farm equipment, etc.

Redwood City Seed Company
P.O. Box 361
Redwood City, CA 94064
(415)325-7333

Sells seeds, live plants by contract, retail and wholesale, mail order. Ships live plants May to August. Catalog $1.00. Native grasses.

Robinett Bulb Farm
P.O. Box 1306
Sebastopol, CA 95473-1306

Sells seeds and bulbs retail, by mail order. Ships September 1 to November 1. Send SASE for catalog. West Coast native bulbs and their seeds.

Tree of Life Nursery
P.O. Box 736
San Juan Capistrano, CA 92693

Sells seeds and live plants wholesale. Ships to Southern California only. Cali-fornia natives only.

Weber Nursery
237 Seeman Drive
Encinitas, CA 92024
(619)753-1661

Sells live plants retail and wholesale, over the counter. California natives only.

Wildflower International, Inc.
918B Enterprise Way
Napa, CA 94558
(707)253-0570

Sells custom-blend seed mixes wholesale. Specializes in native plants.

Wildwood Nursery
3975 Emerald Avenue
La Verne, CA 95452
(714)621-2112

Sells seeds and live plants retail and wholesale, by mail order or phone order. Ships most of the year, U.P.S. available. Catalog $1.00. Specializes in Southwest-ern natives, California drought-tolerant plants. Garden design and consultation.

Idaho

Native Seed Foundation
Star Route G
Moyie Springs, ID 83845

Sells seeds retail and wholesale, by mail order or phone order. Free catalog. Native shrubs.

NORTHPLAN/Mountain Seeds
P.O. Box 9107
Moscow, ID 83843-1607
(208)882-8040

Sells seeds retail and wholesale, by mail order or phone order. Will ship across U.S. and abroad for fee; bulk quantities FOB. Catalog $1.00 refundable; $.50 envelope for native seed list. Specializes in native trees, shrubs, grass, and flowers.

Seeds Blum
Idaho City Stage
Boise, ID 83706

Sells seeds retail by mail order. Will ship if prepaid. Specializes in heirlooms — no hybrids.

Winterfield Ranch Seed Producers
P.O. Box 97
Swan Valley, ID 83449
(208)483-3683

Sells seeds wholesale, by mail order or phone order. Free catalog. Native plants and grasses for the West Coast.

New Mexico

Bernardo Beach Native Plant Farm
Star Route 7, Box 145
Veguita, NM 87062
(505)345-6248

Sells seeds and live plants retail and wholesale, mail order or over the counter. Catalog for 4 First-Class stamps. Specializes in natives of high desert and plains area.

Curtis and Curtis
Star Route 8A
Clovis, NM 88101

Sells seeds retail and wholesale, by phone order. Specializes in native New Mexico grasses and shrubs.

Mesa Garden
P.O. Box 72
Belen, NM 87002
(505)864-3131

Sells seeds and live plants retail, by mail order and phone order. Ships live plants March 1 through December 1, anywhere. Catalog for $.50 SASE. Succulents, cacti.

New Mexico Native Plant Nursery
907 Pope Street
Silver City, NM 88061
(505)538-5201

Sells seeds and plants, retail and wholesale, by mail order and phone order. Native plants. Specializes in Russian olive tree (shipped after November) and drought-resistant plants.

Plants of the Southwest
1812 Second Street
Santa Fe, NM 87501
(505)983-1548

Sells seeds and live plants, retail and wholesale, by mail order, over the counter, and phone order. Catalog $1.50. Specializes in Southwest plants.

Oregon

Callahan Seeds
6045 Foley Lane
Central Point, OR 97502
(503)855-1164

Sells seeds retail and wholesale, by mail order and phone order. Free catalog. Native northwestern American trees, shrubs, and wildflowers. Seeds in packets and bulk.

Goodwin Creek Gardens
P.O. Box 83
Williams, OR 97544

or
154½ Oak Street
Ashland, OR 97520
(503)846-7357

Sells seeds and live plants retail, by mail order, over the counter, and phone order. Ships plants mid-March to mid-June, with some fall shipments. MasterCard and VISA accepted. Catalog $1.00 refundable. Some Southwestern native American plants.

Russel Graham
4030 Eagle Crest Road N.W.
Salem, OR 97304
(503)362-1135

Sells live plants retail and wholesale, by mail order and phone order. Catalog $2.00.

Nature's Garden
Route 1, Box 488
Beaverton, OR 97007
(503)649-6772

Sells live plants, retail and wholesale, by mail order. Catalog $1.75 refundable. Bulk rates available.

Siskiyou Rare Plant Nursery
2825 Cummings Road
Medford, OR 97501
(503)772-6846

Sells live plants retail by mail order. Catalog $2.00. Rock garden and woodland plants of the Northwest.

Botanical Gardens

The following is a list of botanical gardens, arboreta, and nature centers that have gardens or natural areas dedicated to native plants. Many of these organizations provide additional services and have garden shops where books, seeds, and live plants can be purchased.

Arizona

The Arboretum at Flagstaff
P.O. Box 670
South Woody Mountain Road
Flagstaff, AZ 86002
(602)744-1441

Free. Open all year, 10 am–3 pm Mon.–Fri. (open Sat. in summer). Free tours at 11 am and 1 pm. Xeriscape, propagation seminars; occasional lectures. Publishes quarterly newsletter.

Arizona-Sonora Desert Museum
2021 North Kinney Road
Tucson, AZ 85743
(602)883-1380

Entrance fee: $6.00 (adults) $1.00 (children 6–12). Open 8:30am–5 pm Labor Day–Memorial Day; 7:30 am–6 pm in summer. Sells seeds and live plants. Wildflowers, succulents, cacti.

Boyce Thompson Southwestern
   Arboretum
P.O. Box AB
Superior, AZ 85273
(602)689-2811

Entrance fee: $1.50. Open all year, 8 am–5 pm. Sells seeds and live plants. Drought-tolerant plants.

Desert Botanical Garden
1201 North Galvin Parkway
Phoenix, AZ 85008
(602)941-1225

Entrance fee: $3.50 (adults), $3.00 (seniors), $1.00 (children 5–11). Open 9 am–sunset every day. Sells seeds, live plants, and books. Classes and workshops; tourist demonstrations. Wildflower hotline (602)941-2867 March 1–April 30.

Tucson Botanical Gardens
2150 North Alvernon Way
Tucson, AZ 85712
(602)326-9255

Entrance fee $2.00 (adults), $1.50 (seniors). Open all year except holidays, 8 am–4:30 pm. Sells seeds, plants, and books.

California

De Anza College Environmental
   Study Area
21250 Stevens Creek Boulevard
Cupertino, CA 95014
(408)864-8525

Open first Sunday each month 10 am–2 pm, or tours arranged by appointment. Students and older people lead free tours for schools and community. 12 plant communities, several with wildflowers.

Descanso Gardens
1418 Descanso Drive
La Canada, CA 91011
(818)790-5571

Entrance fee: $3.00 adults. Open all year, 9 am–5 pm. Sells live plants.

East Bay Regional Parks Botanic
   Garden
Tilden Regional Park
Berkeley, CA 94708
(415)841-8732

Free. Open all year except major holidays, 8:30 am–5 pm. Sells seeds and live plants. Publishes a journal and garden guide. Native grasses, manzanitas, and native conifers.

Firescapes Demonstration Garden
Santa Barbara Fire Department
121 West Carrillo Street
Santa Barbara, CA 93101
(805)965-5254

Free. Open dawn to dusk every day. Offers classes on planting for public safety.

Fullerton Arboretum
Yorba Linda Boulevard and Associated
   Road
California State Fullerton NE
Fullerton, CA 92634
(714)773-3250

Free. Open all year, every day but holidays 8 am–4:45 pm. Sells seeds, plants, and books. Occasional workshops.

Mendocino Coast Botanic Garden
18220 North Highway 1, P.O. Box 1143
Fort Bragg, CA 95437

Entrance fee: $5.00 (adults), $4.00 (seniors), $3.00 (children). Open every day but Christmas and New Year's Day, 9 am–5 pm (summer), 10 am–4 pm (winter). Small library; tours upon request.

Hortense Miller Garden
2511 All View Terrace
Laguna Beach, CA 92657
(714)494-6740

Free. Open Tues.–Sat., noon–dusk.

The Living Desert
47-900 S. Portola Avenue
Palm Desert, CA 92260
(619)346-5694

Entrance fee: $5.00 adults, $4.50 seniors, $2.00 children. Open Sept. 1–June 15, 9 am–5 pm. Sells seeds and live plants. Eight different desert regions represented.

Los Angeles State and
   County Arboretum
301 N. Baldwin Avenue
Arcadia, CA 91007-2697
(818)446-8251

Entrance fee: $3.00 adults, $1.50 children. Open all year, 9 am–4:30 pm. Sells seeds and live plants.

Lummis Garden Project,
   Historical Society of
   Southern California
200 East Avenue 43
Los Angeles, CA 90031
(213)222-0546

Free. Open Wed.–Sun. 1 pm–4 pm. Residential model for water conservation.

Moorten Botanical Garden
1701 South Palm Canyon Drive
Palm Springs, CA 92264
(619)327-6555

Entrance fee: $1.50 (adult), $.50 (child). Open Mon.–Sat. 9 am–4:30 pm, Sun. 10 am–4 pm. Sells seeds, live plants, and books.

Pacific Grove Museum of
   Natural History
165 Forest Avenue
Pacific Grove, CA 93950

Free. Open Tues–Sun. 10 am–5 pm. Sells seeds, live plants, and books. Native plants of Monterey County.

Theodore Payne Foundation
10459 Tuxford Street
Sun Valley, CA 91352
(818)768-1802

Free. Sells seeds, live plants, and books. Demonstration garden, wildflower garden.

Quail Botanical Gardens
220 Quail Gardens Drive
Encinitas, CA 92024
(619)436-3036

Entrance fee: $1.00 per car. Open all year, 8 am–5 pm. Sells seeds, live plants, and books. Public and children's tours of native plant areas; special interest programs.

Rancho Santa Ana Botanical Garden
1500 N. College Avenue
Claremont, CA 91711
(714)625-8767

Free. Open all year, except holidays, 8 am–5 pm. Sells live plants. Several different native plant gardens.

Regional Parks Botanic Garden
Tilden Regional Park
Berkeley, CA 94708-1199
(415)841-8732

Free. Open all year, except holidays, 8:30 am–5 pm, 8:30 am–6 pm (summer). Sells seeds and live plants.

Santa Barbara Botanic Garden
1212 Mission Canyon Road
Santa Barbara, CA 93105
(805)682-4726

Open every day, 8 am–dusk. Sells seeds, live plants, and books. Calendar and newsletter for members. Tours and classes ongoing. Library, research facility. Member of Master Garden California Certificate Program with University of California Cooperative Extension.

South Coast Botanic Garden
26300 Crenshaw Boulevard
Palos Verdes Peninsula, CA 91011
(213)544-1847

Entrance fee: $3.00 adults. Open all year, 9 am–4:30 pm. Sells seeds and live plants.

Strybing Arboretum and Botanic
   Garden
Golden Gate Park; 9th Avenue
   at Lincoln Way
San Francisco, CA 94122
(415)662-1316

Free. Open every day, 8 am–4 pm (weekdays), 10 am–5 pm (weekends). Sells seeds, live plants, and books. Library.

University Arboretum
University of California at Davis
Davis, CA 95616
(916)752-2498

Free. Open all year, daylight hours. Sells seeds and live plants.

University of California/
   Berkeley Botanical Garden
Centennial Drive
Berkeley, CA 94720
(415)643-8040

Free. Open every day but Christmas, 8:45 am–4:45 pm. Sells live plants and books. Lectures, field trips for small fee.

Mary S. Whitaker Memorial Garden
Torrey Pines State Reserve
La Jolla, CA 92038
(619)454-1444

Admission charged to Torrey Pines State Reserve. Open 8 am–10 pm (summer), 8 am–5 pm (winter).

Nevada

Botanical Garden
Ethel M. Chocolate Factory
2 Cactus Drive
Henderson, NV 89014
(702)458-8864

Free. Open every day 8:30 am–6 pm. Sells seeds, live plants, and books. Field trips.

New Mexico

Living Desert State Park
P.O. Box 100
Carlsbad, NM 88220
(505)887-5516

Entrance fee: $3.00; group and educational rates. Open 8 am–8 pm (summer), 9 am–5 pm (winter). Sells seeds, live plants, and books.

University of New Mexico,
   Physical Plants Department
Albuquerque, NM 87131
(505)277-2421

Free. About 5 acres of wildflowers and cacti on premises.

Oregon

The Berry Botanic Garden
11505 SW Summerville Avenue
Portland, OR 97219
(503)636-4112

Entrance fee: $15 annual membership. Open all year, by appointment only, Mon.–Fri. Call for appointment. Programs on native plants for members.

Leach Botanical Gardens
6704 Southeast 122nd Avenue
Portland, OR 97236
(503)761-9503

Free. Open all year, Tues.–Sun., 10 am–5 pm. Sells seeds, live plants, and books. Emphasis on native Northwestern plants.

Mt. Pisgah Arboretum
P.O. Box 5621
Howard Buford Recreation Area
Eugene, OR 97405
(503)747-3817

Free. Open all year, daylight hours. Publishes bimonthly newsletter. Sells seeds, live plants, and books.

Utah

Red Butte Gardens and Arboretum at
   the University of Utah
Building 436, University of Utah
Salt Lake City, UT 84112
(801)581-5322

Open every day but Christmas, 9 am–sunset. Sells seeds, live plants, and books. Slide library.

Utah Botanical Gardens
1817 North Main Street
Farmington, UT 84025
(801)581-5322

Free. Open all year, daylight hours. Sells books. Display and research garden, emphasis on annuals.

Native Plant and Horticultural Societies

This is a listing of native plant societies, botanical organizations, and horticultural societies that are interested in native plants.

Arizona

Arizona Heritage Program
Arizona Game & Fish Department
2222 West Greenway Road
Phoenix, AZ 85023
(602)942-3000

Arizona Native Plant Society
P.O. Box 41206 Sun Station
Tucson, AZ 85717
Publishes The Plant Press. *Six chapters in the state.*

Center for Plant Conservation
c/o The Arboretum at Flagstaff
South Woody Mountain Road
P.O. Box 670
Flagstaff, AZ 86002
(602)744-1441

Center for Plant Conservation
c/o Desert Botanical Garden
1201 North Galvin Parkway
Phoenix, AZ 85008
(602)941-1225

The Nature Conservancy
Arizona Field Office
300 East University Boulevard, Suite 230
Tucson, AZ 85705
(602)622-3861

California

California Native Plant Society
909 12th Street, #116
Sacramento, CA 95814
(916)447-2677
Publishes Freemontia *and several books.*

California Nongame-Heritage Program
The Resources Agency
Department of Fish & Game
1416 9th Street, 12th floor
Sacramento, CA 95814
(916)322-2493

Center for Plant Conservation
c/o University of California/
   Berkeley Botanical Garden
Centennial Drive
Berkeley, CA 94720
(415)643-8040

Cuyamaca Botanical Society
Cuyamaca College
2950 Jamacha Road
El Cajon, CA 92019-4304
(619)670-3544

The Nature Conservancy
California Field Office
785 Market Street
San Francisco, CA 94103
(415)777-0487

Theodore Payne Foundation
10459 Tuxford Street
Sun Valley, CA 91352
(818)768-1802
Publishes Quarterly.

Southern California Botanists
California State University
   Department of Biology
Fullerton, CA 92634
(714)449-7034
Publishes Crossosoma.

Idaho

Idaho Native Plant Society
Box 9451
Boise, ID 83707
(208)375-8740
Publishes Sage Notes.

Idaho Natural Heritage Program
Department of Fish & Game
600 South Walnut Street, Box 25
Boise, ID 83707
(208)334-3402

The Nature Conservancy
Idaho Field Office
P.O. Box 64
Sun Valley, ID 83353
(208)726-3007

Nevada

Nevada Natural Heritage Program
Department of Conservation &
   Natural Resources
c/o Division of State Parks
Capitol Complex, Nye Building
201 South Fall Street
Carson City, NV 89710
(702)885-4370

Northern Nevada Native Plant
Society
Box 8965
Reno, NV 89507
Publishes Mentzelia *and a newsletter.*

New Mexico

Native Plant Society of New Mexico
P.O. Box 5917
Santa Fe, NM 87502

New Mexico Natural Resources
Survey Section
Villagra Building
Santa Fe, NM 87503
(505)827-7862
Publishes Native Plant Society of New
Mexico Newsletter.

The Nature Conservancy
New Mexico Field Office
107 Cienega Street
Santa Fe, NM 87501
(505)988-3867

Oregon

Native Plant Society of Oregon
c/o Department of Biology
Southern Oregon State College
Ashland, OR 97520
Publishes Bulletin. *Regional chapters.*

The Nature Conservancy
Oregon Field Office
1205 N.W. 25th Avenue
Portland, OR 97210
(503)228-9561

Oregon Natural Heritage Program
Oregon Field Office
1205 N.W. 25th Avenue
Portland, OR 97201
(503)229-5078

Utah

Center for Plant Conservation
State Arboretum of Utah
Building 436, University of Utah
(801)581-5322

The Nature Conservancy
Great Basin Field Office
P.O. Box 11486, Pioneer Station Salt
Lake City, UT 84102
(801)531-0999

Utah Native Plant Society
P.O. Box 52041
Salt Lake City, UT 84152-0041
(801)581-5322
Publishes The Sego Lily.

Utah Natural Heritage Program
3 Triad Center, Suite 400
Salt Lake City, UT 84180-1204
(801)538-5524

Washington

The Nature Conservancy
Washington Field Office
1601 Second Avenue, Suite 910
Seattle, WA 98101
(206)728-9696

Operation Wildflower
State Chapter
1416 170th Place Northeast
Bellevue, WA 98008
(206)747-0268

Washington Native Plant Society
c/o Department of Botany, KB-15
University of Washington
Seattle, WA 98195
(206)543-1942
Publishes Douglasia. *Six chapters.*

Washington Natural Heritage Program
Department of Natural Resources
Mail Stop EX-13
Olympia, WA 98504
(206)753-2448

National Organizations

American Horticultural Society
7931 East Boulevard Drive
Alexandria, VA 22308
(703)768-5700
Publishes American Horticulturalist.

American Rock Garden Society
c/o Buffy Parker
15 Fairmead Road
Darien, CT 06820
(203)655-2750
Publishes The Bulletin of the American Rock Garden Society. *Twenty-
nine chapters in North America.*

Center for Plant Conservation
125 Arbor Way
Jamaica Plain, MA 02130
(617)524-6988

Conservation Foundation/
World Wildlife Fund
1250 24th Street N.W.
Suite 500
Washington, DC 20037
(202)293-4800

Environmental Defense Fund
444 Park Avenue South
New York, NY 10016
(212)686-4191

National Wildflower Research Center
2600 FM 973 North
Austin, TX 78725
(512)929-3600
Publishes Wildflower.

The Nature Conservancy
Western Regional Office
785 Market Street
San Francisco, CA 94103
(415)777-0541

Operation Wildflower
National Council of State Garden
Clubs
Mrs. C. Norman Collard, Chairman
Box 860
Pocasset, MA 02559
Publishes Columbine. *State and regional
chapters. Works with Department of
Transportation to plant wildflowers along
highways.*

Soil and Water Conservation Society
7515 Northeast Ankeny Road
Ankeny, IA 50021
(515)289-2331

U.S. Fish & Wildlife Service
Office of Endangered Species
Washington, DC 20240
(703)235-2771

Xeriscaping Council, Inc.
P.O. Box 11672
Austin, TX 78716-3172
(512)392-6225

Publishes Xeriscape News. *State branches; 36 state educational programs.*

APPENDIX D
References

Art, H.W., 1986. *A Garden of Wildflowers*. Garden Way Publishing/ Storey Communications, Pownal, VT. 290 pp.

An illustrated guide to 101 native North American species and how to grow them.

Art, H.W., 1988. *Creating a Wildflower Meadow*. Garden Way Publishing, Pownal, VT. 32 pp.

A Garden Way Publishing Bulletin on grasses and wildflowers suitable for North American meadows.

Bailey, L.H., 1935. *The Standard Cyclopedia of Horticulture*. MacMillan, New York, NY. 3639 pp.

A classic gardening encyclopedia containing information on numerous native wildflowers as well as domesticated species.

Bakker, E., 1971. *An Island Called California*. U. California Press, Berkeley, CA. 361 pp.

A superb, readable introduction to the various types of vegetation in California.

California Department of Water Resources, 1981. *Plants for California Landscapes*. Bulletin 209. The State of California Resources Agency, Department of Water Resources, Sacramento, CA. 139 pp.

Inexpensive, yet packed with information about native and exotic trees, shrubs, vines, and wildflowers suitable for droughty conditions.

California Native Plant Society, 1977. *Native Plants: A Viable Option*. California Native Plant Society, Sacramento, CA. 213 pp.

Suggestions for gardening with native plants.

Collard, L.R.,ed., 1985. *Wildflower Culture Guide*. National Council of State Garden Clubs, Inc., St. Louis, MO. 44 pp.

Articles on wildflower culture, wildflower gardens, and "Operation Wildflower."

Crockett, J.U. & O.E. Allen, 1977. *Wildflower Gardening*. Time-Life Books, Alexandria, VA. 160 pp.

Coast-to-coast examples of natives for the garden, with color illustrations.

Emery, D.E., 1988. *Seed Propagation of Native California Plants*. Santa Barbara Botanic Garden, Santa Barbara, CA. 118 pp.

An excellent book listing many native woody and herbaceous plants with recommended treatments for seed germination.

Hartmann, H.T. & D.E. Kester, 1975. *Plant Propagation*, 3rd ed. Prentice-Hall, Englewood Cliffs, NJ. 662 pp.

A standard text about plant propagation.

Hill, L., 1985. *Secrets of Plant Propagation*. Garden Way Publishing, Pownal, VT. 168 pp.

How to propagate woody and herbaceous plants.

Hull, H.S., ed., 1982. *Handbook on Gardening with Wildflowers*. Brooklyn Botanic Garden, Brooklyn, NY. [B.B.G. Plants & Gardens 18 (1).] 85 pp.

A variety of articles about native plant gardening.

Jacob, W. & I. Jacob, 1985. *Gardens of North America and Hawaii*. Timber Press, Portland, OR. 368 pp.

A useful cross-continent guide to gardens and arboreta with short descriptions and helpful state maps.

Johnson, L.B. & C.B. Less, 1988. *Wildflowers Across America*. National Wildflower Research Center & Abbeyville Press, New York, NY. 309 pp.

A coffee-table book with exciting and elegant color photographs of native and exotic wildflowers.

Labadie, E. 1978. *Native Plants for Use in the California Landscape*. Sierra City Press, Sierra City, CA. 256 pp.

Lenz, L., 1973. *Native Plants for California Gardens*. Rancho Santa Ana Botanic Garden, Claremont, CA. 176 pp.

Martin, A.C., H.S. Zim, & A.L. Nelson, 1951. *American Wildlife and Plants*. Dover, New York, NY. 500 pp.

While not a book about wildflower gardening, this book is quite helpful in planning gardens to attract various wildlife species.

Martin, L.C. 1986. *The Wildflower Meadow Book*. East Woods Press, Charlotte, N.C. 303 pp.

A coast-to-coast treatment of native and exotic wildflowers that grow in fields and meadows.

McGourty, F., 1978. *Ground Covers and Vines*. Brooklyn Botanic Garden, Brooklyn, NY. [B.B.G. *Plants & Gardens*, 32 (3).] 80 pp.

A useful booklet with articles on both native and exotic plants used as ground covers.

Munz, P.A., 1961. *California Spring Wildflowers*. U. California Press, Berkeley, CA. 122 pp.

Guide to the common spring wildflowers from the base of the Sierra Nevada and southern mountains to the Pacific Coast, some illustrated with color photographs.

Munz, P.A., 1962. *California Desert Wildflowers*. U. California Press, Berkeley, CA. 122 pp.

Guide to the common southwestern desert wildflowers, some illustrated with color photographs.

Munz, P.A., 1964. *Shore Wildflowers*. U. California Press, Berkeley, CA. 122 pp.

Guide to the Pacific Coast wildflowers, some illustrated with color photographs.

National Wildflower Research Center, 1989. *Wildflower Handbook*. Texas Monthly Press, Austin, TX. pp 337.

A very useful reference on wildflowers, where to purchase them, and where to obtain further information about them.

Niehaus, T.F. & C.L. Ripper, 1976. *A Field Guide to Pacific States Wildflowers*. Houghton Mifflin, Boston, MA. 432 pp.

The Peterson Field Guide Series edition for California to Washington and east to Utah.

Niehaus, T.F., C.L. Ripper, & V. Savage, 1984. *A Field Guide to Southwestern and Texas Wildflowers*. Houghton Mifflin, Boston, MA. 449 pp.

The Peterson Field Guide Series edition for Texas to Arizona and north to Colorado.

Ornduff, R, 1974. *An Introduction to California Plant Life*. U. California Press, Berkeley, CA. 152 pp.

An excellent short guide to the diverse plant communities of California.

Parsons, M.E., 1966. *The Wild Flowers of California*. Dover, New York, NY. 425 pp.

A reprint of the 1907 classic covering 666 different native southwestern species, some with elegant illustrations.

Phillips, J., 1987. *Southwestern Landscaping with Native Plants*. Museum of N.M. Press, Santa Fe, NM. 140 pp.

A helpful guide to planning and executing xeriscapes in the Southwest.

Ray, M.H. & R.P. Nicholls, 1988. *The Traveler's Guide to American Gardens*. U. North Carolina Press, Chapel Hill, NC. 375 pp.

A state-by-state guide to gardens in the United States.

Saratoga Horticultural Foundation, 1982. *Selected California Native Plants with Commercial Sources*. Saratoga Horticultural Foundation, Inc., Saratoga, CA. 72 pp.

A booklet featuring woody and herba-

ceous natives, their cultural requirements, and where to purchase them.

Schmidt, M.G., 1980. *Growing California Native Plants*. U. California Press, Berkeley, CA. 366 pp.

A comprehensive treatment of California wildflowers and woody perennials. A classic.

Steffek, E.F., 1983. *The New Wild Flowers and How to Grow Them*. Timber Press, Portland, OR. 186 pp.

A sampling of wildflowers from North America, with useful tables of species from various regions and habitats.

Sullivan, G.A. & R.H. Dailey, 1981. *Resources on Wildflower Propagation*. National Council of State Garden Clubs, Inc., St. Louis, MO. 331 pp.

A bargain at $3.00. Contains a wealth of technical information about plants native to various regions of the U.S.

Sunset Books, 1988. *Western Garden Book*. Lane Publishing, Menlo Park, CA. 592 pp.

An excellent resource book for gardeners from the Rockies to the Pacific. Treats both native and exotic species with great care.

Taylor, R.J. & R.W. Valum, 1974. *Wildflowers 2: Sagebrush Country*. Touchstone Press, Beaverton, OR. 143 pp.

A color photographic guide to the wildflowers of the Great Basin area.

Wilson, W.H.W., 1984. *Landscaping with Wildflowers and Native Plants*. Ortho Books, San Francisco, CA. 96 pp.

Listings of native plants for various regions and habitats.

Young, J.A. & C.G. Young, 1986. *Collecting, Processing, and Germinating Seeds of Wildland Plants*. Timber Press, Portland, OR. 236 pp.

Glossary

Annual. A plant whose life cycle from seed to mature plant, producing flowers, fruits and seeds, is completed in a single growing season. After seeds are produced, the plant usually dies.

Anther. A pollen-producing sac attached to the filament in the male portion of a flower.

Axil. The point of attachment between stem and leaf.

Basal rosette. An arrangement of leaves radiating from a short stem at the ground surface. Most biennials have a rosette form during their first growing season.

Biennial. A plant whose life cycle extends over two growing seasons. The first year the seed germinates, producing a seedling that usually remains short over the winter. The second growing season the seedling rapidly elongates, flowers, produces seeds, and then dies.

Bolting. The rapid elongation and flowering of biennials during their second growing season.

Boreal. Pertaining to regions of the northern hemisphere that have cold winters and forests dominated by coniferous species.

Bract. A modified leaflike structure, often resembling a petal, surrounding a flower or flower cluster.

Bulb. A fleshy rootstock composed of leaf bases or scaly leaves.

Bunch grasses. Species of grass that form distinct clumps or bunches as they grow, in contrast to the sod-forming grasses usually grown for lawns.

Calyx. The collective term for the sepals of a flower.

Capsule. A dry fruit that splits open to release its seeds.

Chaparral. Thickets of fire-adapted shrubs and small trees that develop in regions with hot dry summers and mild wet winters.

Charate. The charred remains of burned chaparral plants.

Coastal prairie. A natural grassland that develops near the Pacific Coast, usually on south-facing slopes that burn frequently.

Complete flowers. Flowers with sepals, petals, stamens, and a pistil all present.

Composite flower. A flower made up of many individual florets clustered into a common head, as is typical in members of the aster family.

Compound leaf. A leaf that is divided into two or more separate leaflets.

Corm. A fleshy rootstock formed by a short, thick, underground stem.

Corolla. The collective term for the petals of a flower.

Crest. A ridge of tissue.

Deciduous. Pertaining to plant parts, usually leaves, that are shed annually.

Desert. An ecosystem that develops in regions with annual precipitation of less than 10 inches, usually dominated by widely spaced shrubs and, where winters are mild, succulent species.

Disc flower (disc floret). One of the small, tubular flowers that form the central disc of flower heads in many members of the aster family.

Dissected. Deeply divided or split into lobes.

Dormancy. The resting or inactive phase of plants or seeds. Dormancy of shoots is usually in response to unfavorable environmental conditions. The breaking of seed dormancy requires moisture and sometimes cold tempertures and abrasion of the seed coat.

Elaiosome. An oily, starchy appendage on some seeds that attracts ants and other insects, which act as disperal agents.

Entire. A leaf margin that is smooth and lacking teeth.

Fibrous roots. A root system with many thin or branched root elements.

Filament. The anther-bearing stalk of a stamen.

Firescaping. A landscaping technique in which fire-resistant species are planted in close proximity to dwellings and other structures in fire-prone regions.

Floret. One of the small flowers that is clustered together forming the composite flower head in members of the aster family. Florets may be either tubular disc florets or straplike ray florets.

Flowering shoot. A stem that produces flowers.

Flower head. A cluster of florets or small flowers gathered together on a common receptacle, typically found in members of the aster family.

Forcing. Inducing a perennial to flower out of season. Forcing often involves artificial chilling followed by warming the plant.

Germination. The breaking of dormancy in seeds or the sprouting of pollen grains deposited on a stigma.

Habitat. The kind of environment inhabited by a particular species.

Half-hardy. An annual plant that is sown in early spring and flowers in summer.

Hardiness zone. An index relating geographic regions to a plant's ability to withstand minimum winter temperatures. Hardiness zones developed by the U.S. Department of Agriculture range from zone 1, with a minimum temperature of $-50\,°F$, to zone 10, with minimum temperatures of 30 to $40\,°F$.

Hardy annual. An annual plant whose seeds can withstand subfreezing winter temperatures and whose seedlings can withstand spring frosts.

Hardy perennial. A perennial plant that is not permanently injured or killed by subfreezing temperatures.

Herbaceous. Plants that lack woody tissues and therefore "die back" to the soil surface at the end of the growing season.

Humus. Soft brown or black amorphous substance formed through the decomposition of leaves, wood, and other organic materials.

Innoculant. A commercially formulated strain of rhizobium added to the soil to aid in the establishment of various members of the bean family.

Inoculation. The addition of rhizobia to the soil.

Involucre. A whorl of leafy bracts surrounding composite flower heads such as those in the aster family.

Keel. The lower, pouchlike lip of flowers of certain members of the bean family. The keel is formed by the fusion of two petals.

Leaflets. The individual segments of a compound leaf.

Legume. A dry, flattened pod fruit that splits open at both edges when mature, as is found in members of the bean family. The term is also applied to the species of the bean family.

Long-day plant. A plant that flowers in response to the short nights of late spring and early summer.

Moist chilling treatment. A means of enhancing the germination of some seeds by storing them under moist conditions at low temperatures prior to planting them.

Montane. Pertaining to mountain environments, usually below the timberline.

Nodules. Outgrowths on the roots of plants in the bean family that are inhabited by nitrogen-fixing microorganisms known as rhizobia.

Non-flowering shoot. A stem that does not produce flowers; a vegetative shoot.

Ovary. The swollen base of a pistil, containing ovules. The ripening ovary, which is sometimes fused to the receptacle, becomes the fruit.

Ovules. The female sex cells that become seeds following fertilization.

Palmate. A pattern of compound leaflets or leaf venation, with elements radiating from a central point.

Peduncle. The main flowering stalk of a plant.

Perennial. A plant whose life cycle extends for an indefinite period beyond two growing seasons. These plants generally do not die following flowering.

Perfect flowers. Flowers with both stamens and a pistil, but lacking either sepals and/or petals.

Petal. A modified leaf attached to the receptacle outside the stamens and inside the calyx. Petals are usually showy and serve to attract pollinators to the flower.

Petiole. The stalk that attaches a leaf to a stem.

pH. A measure of the acidity/alkalinity of a substance ranging from 0 (strongly acidic) to 14 (strongly alkaline), with 7 being neutral.

Pistil. The female sexual part of a flower, consisting of the stigma, style, and ovary.

Plugs. A method of propagation by planting individual seeds in specially designed trays with small indentations. The root system of the seedlings fills the hole, forming a plug that can be easily removed and planted where desired.

Pollen. The powdery material produced in anthers, containing the male sex cells of flowering plants.

Pollination. The transfer of pollen from an anther to a stigma.

Propagation. Increasing the numbers of plants through seeds, cuttings, or divisions.

Pulvinus. A small, bulbous organ at the base of a petiole that controls the sun-tracking movement of leaves.

Ray flower (ray floret). One of the small flowers with a straplike petal, usually arranged in rings around the margin of flower heads in members of the aster family.

Receptacle. The fleshy tissue at the tip of a flower stalk to which flower parts are attached. Different species may have receptacles that are positioned below the ovary, form a cup around the ovary, or completely enclose the ovary.

Rhizobia. Microorganisms that inhabit nodules on the roots of members of the bean family. These organisms have the ability to take nitrogen from the air and create nitrogen compounds, usable by their host plants.

Rhizome. A horizontal, usually branched, underground stem with buds and roots.

Root division. Propagating plants by cutting vertically between root segments.

Root rot. Plant diseases, usually caused by fungi, that lead to the degeneration of roots.

Rootstock. An underground stem of a perennial plant with its associated buds and roots.

Runner. A thin, creeping, horizontal stem that trails along the surface of the ground and gives rise to small plants.

Scape. A leafless stem bearing a cluster of flowers.

Scarification. Abrasion of the seed coat allowing the passage of water and oxygen into the seed, thereby enhancing germination in some species.

Seed coat. The outer protective covering of a seed.

Sepal. A modified leaf that forms the covering of a flower bud. Sepals are attached to the outer margin of the receptacle and are usually green. However, in some species the sepals are brightly colored and resemble petals.

Shoot. The aboveground or stem portion of a plant that bears leaves, buds, and flowers.

Shoot bud. A bud that develops into stem and leaf tissue.

Short-day plant. A plant that flowers in response to the long nights of fall or early spring.

Simple flower. A solitary flower borne on a single stem.

Slip. An old-fashioned name for a cutting used for propagation.

Sods. A method of propagation by densely planting seeds in flats or trays. The root systems of the seedlings intertwine, allowing the sod to be removed in a single piece and planted where desired.

Softwood cutting. A propagation technique of cutting green, rapidly growing portions of stems while they are pliable.

Spadix. A fleshy, spindle-shaped column bearing flowers in members of the arum family.

Spathe. A large, leafy bract that frequently envelops the spadix in members of the arum and other plant families.

Stamen. The male sexual part of a flower consisting of an anther and a filament.

Stigma. The top surface of a pistil upon which pollen grains are deposited.

Stolon. A thin, underground runner.

Stratification. Chilling seeds to enhance their germination.

Style. The portion of the pistil connecting the stigma and the ovary.

Taproot. A thick, strongly vertical root, usually extending to considerable depth, for example, the carrot.

Tender annual. An annual plant whose seedlings are killed by spring frosts.

Tender perennial. Perennial plants that are permanently damaged or killed by subfreezing temperatures.

True root. The descending, underground portion of a plant that is specialized to provide support and absorb water and nutrients. True roots usually lack buds.

Tuber. A rootstock formed by a fleshy, swollen tip of a stolon.

Tule meadow. Wetland vegetation interspersed in valley grasslands and dominated by tule (bulrush) and cattails.

Vernal pools. "Hog wallows" or depressions that collect water over the winter rainy season and form temporary pools. As pools dry out over the spring various wildflowers bloom at their edges.

Vernalization. The cold treatment needed by some fall-germinating plants to promote flowering the following spring.

Weed. Any plant that grows where it is not wanted.

Wetlands. An area of low-lying land with soils that are submerged or wet for a significant portion of each year.

Wildflower. An herbaceous plant capable of growing, reproducing, and becoming established without cultivation.

Winter annual. An annual plant that usually germinates in the fall, overwinters as a seedling, and flowers the following spring.

Woody. Having hard, tough tissues that persist from year to year and are capable of producing shoot or flower buds. Woody plants also have the capacity to increase in diameter from year to year.

Xeriscaping. A landscaping technique in which water consumption is reduced by planting drought-resistant species, matching water requirements of landscape plants to available soil moisture, using high-efficiency irrigation systems, and other water-conserving techniques.

Index

Boldface numbers, such as **55**, indicate that illustrations or tables appear on that page.